EXPLORING
MY WORLD

By Lynn Cohen
Illustrated by Susan Pinkerton

Publisher: Roberta Suid
Editor: Bonnie Bernstein
Cover Design: David Hale
Design and Production: Susan Pinkerton
Cover art: Corbin Hillam

m⬤nday morning®

Monday Morning is a registered trademark
of Monday Morning Books, Inc.

ISBN 0-912107-47-2

Printed in the United States of America

9 8 7 6 5 4 3 2 1

CONTENTS

INTRODUCTION

Three-, four-, and five-year-olds explore their everyday worlds with intense energy and imagination. And what do they find? Much to love, much to worry about or fear, and much to celebrate.

Exploring My World is a collection of art, music, and movement activities grouped around early childhood themes. These ideas are appropriate for preschoolers in the following settings:

- nursery schools and preschools
- public and private kindergartens
- parents and children at home
- daycare facilities (centers or homes)
- theater arts programs
- library programs

Exploring My World is divided into three chapters. Chapter One, "Children Are a Part of Families," explores a child's relationships with his or her parents, brothers and sisters, grandparents, and babysitter. Acknowledging that in these modern times families and households are different, *Exploring My World* offers suggestions for adapting or reinterpreting ideas so that they work equally well for children in various circumstances.

Chapter Two, "Children Have Fun," explores a variety of fun and festive themes — friends, parties, the circus, and going camping. Chapter Three, "Children Wonder," explores some of the apprehensions children feel as they encounter stressful situations, like being sick, moving, having trouble sleeping at night, or as they begin to develop greater independence by starting school and learning to stay safe.

To begin a unit, read aloud books from the recommended reading list, then follow up with an art activity and a song or creative movement. Art activities include a list of readily available materials, necessary preparation, and a detailed description of what the children do. Continue a theme for a day or a week; there is plenty of material in each unit, and you are likely to come up with ideas of your own as well.

Share your children's loves, fears, and festivities with this collection of activities. Then use *Exploring My World* as a model for developing your own integrated curriculum around themes that will appeal to your children.

Chapter One:

Children Are a Part of Families

MOTHERS AND FATHERS

Children three to five years old want more than anything to be like their mommies and daddies. Today, more than half the mothers of children in this age group are in the work force. For these children, being like mommy includes going to work, and being like daddy means sharing the household chores.

All families are different, however, and many families change. Some households grow larger when a new baby is born, or when a stepsister or grandparent comes to live with the family. Some households grow smaller when parents separate or a grandparent dies. Whenever necessary, follow the suggestions for adapting activities to accommodate children who live in less traditional households.

ART ACTIVITIES

FAMILY MOBILE

Materials: Sticks, string, construction paper, crayons (or magazines or family photos), scissors, hole punch.
Preparation: Suspend strings from one long stick to a couple of shorter sticks, and hang more string from the shorter sticks to make a mobile.
Activity: Children draw pictures of family members on construction paper, cut them out, and punch holes in the tops. Tie a string on the mobile to each picture. *Note: If the children are too young to draw figures, help them make a mobile using photographs or magazine cutouts of people resembling family members.*

Families are different: Encourage children to include stepfamily members, a grandparent or housekeeper, pets, and anyone else in their immediate household. Children who spend time in two different households can make two mobiles.

DADDY AND MOMMY

Materials: Two paper bowls, stapler, yarn, felt scraps, construction paper, glue.
Preparation: Staple the rims of the bowls together.
Activity: The child glues the facial features of Mommy on one side and Daddy on the other side. The child can cut eyes, noses, mouths, and ears out of felt or paper, and use snips of yarn for hair.

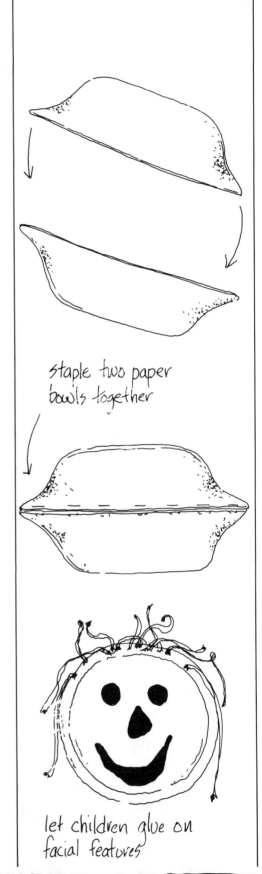

staple two paper bowls together

let children glue on facial features

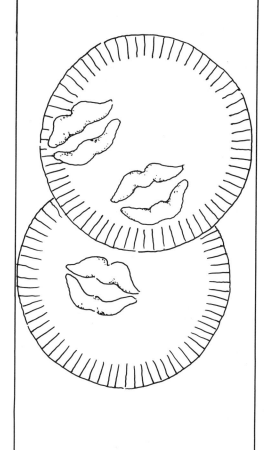

Families are different: A child who has two sets of parents (natural and stepparents) can make two double-sided figures. A child with a single parent or separated parents might be more comfortable making single-sided figures.

GOODNIGHT KISSES FOR MOM AND DAD

Materials: Lipstick, mirror, paper plate.
Activity: Help children put on lipstick in front of a mirror. The children kiss a paper plate to make prints. They give their kiss prints to their parents.

Families are different: Provide extra plates so children whose parents are separated can make each parent a collage of kisses. A child who lives with one parent and misses living with the other may feel strongly about giving kisses to the absent parent.

DAD'S OR MOM'S BRIEFCASE

Materials: Brown lunch-size paper bag, scissors, stapler, leather scraps (ask at a shoe repair store).
Preparation: Cut down the paper bag to a height of about five inches. Save the scrap.
Activity: Children fold the scrap from the paper bag in half and cut out two handles at once. Staple a handle at the top of both sides of the bag. Then the children can glue leather scraps all over their briefcases.

Families are different: Not all children have Moms or Dads who carry papers to work in a briefcase. The same construction can be called a pocketbook or suitcase.

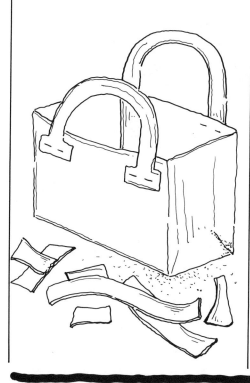

COLORING KEYS

Materials: Variety of keys from Mom's pocketbook or Dad's pockets, white construction paper, crayons.
Preparation: Peel the paper labels off the crayons.
Activity: Children arrange the keys on a table. They lay their papers over the keys and rub over the surfaces with different crayons. Colorful impressions, or "rubbings," of the keys will appear on the paper.

MOMMY AND DADDY WORK

Materials: Brown wrapping paper, black marker, magazines, scissors, glue.
Preparation: Cut off a large piece of wrapping paper. Write the heading Mommy and Daddy Work across the top.
Activity: Children look through magazines and cut out pictures of people doing the kind of work their own parents do, including housework. They paste the pictures on the mural.

A WALLET LIKE MOMMY'S OR DADDY'S

Materials: Construction paper, color markers, play money, child's photo.

Preparation: To make a paper wallet, letter-fold a piece of construction paper. Unfold the top panel, then staple the other two together along the sides. Fold over the top panel again. For a man's wallet (billfold style), fold the wallet in half.

Activity: Children decorate their wallets with colored markers, then place play money and a photo of themselves (that Mommy or Daddy shows to other people) inside.

fold and staple

PAPIER MACHE MOM OR DAD

Materials: Newspapers, string, wallpaper paste, water, container for paste, paint, paintbrushes, shellac, plastic eyes with moving eyeballs (available at craft stores), yarn, fabric scraps, glue.

Preparation: Roll up several rolls of newspaper. Fasten them with string to form a figure. Mix the wallpaper paste in warm water until you have a thin creamy paste. Rip more newspaper into strips.

Activity: Children soak newspaper strips in the paste mixture and wrap them around their figure bases. After the figures are covered with three layers of strips, let them dry thoroughly for several days. Then let the children paint their figures to look like Mom or Dad. They can also glue on moving eyeballs, yarn hair, and clothes cut out of fabric scraps.

form figure, then wrap with soaked newspaper

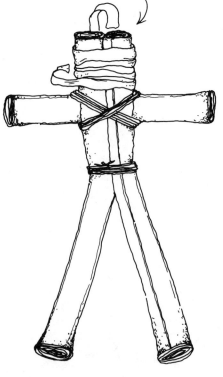

SILHOUETTE FOR MOTHER'S DAY

Materials: Black and white construction paper, white chalk, film projector, scissors, glue.

Preparation: Hang black construction paper on a wall. Set the projector on a table and focus on the black paper hanging on the wall.

Activity: Children sit on a chair one at a time so that you can see the profiles of their faces. Focus the projector on the child's profile. Draw the profile with white chalk on the black paper. Have the children cut out their silhouettes and glue them on white paper. Frame the silhouettes with real or homemade frames.

ODDS-AND-ENDS BOX FOR FATHER'S DAY

Materials: Small wooden box or cigar box, cancelled stamps, glue, shellac, brush for applying shellac.

Activity: Children glue stamps all over the box, overlapping them. Help the children shellac the boxes after the glue dries.

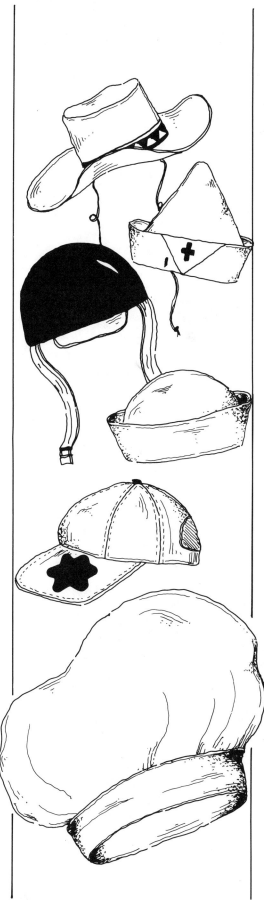

MUSIC AND MOVEMENT ACTIVITIES

SONG: "This Is the Way We Do Our Work"

Sing these verses to the tune of "Here We Go Round the Mulberry Bush."

> This is the way we sweep the floor
> Sweep the floor, sweep the floor.
> This is the way we sweep the floor
> When we help Mom and Dad.

Other verses:

> This is the way we vacuum the rug. . .
> This is the way we wash the windows. . .
> This is the way we dust the furniture. . .
> This is the way we make our beds. . .

WORK HATS

Collect hats worn by workers in different occupations, including the occupations of the children's parents. Put all the hats in a bag. The children take turns pulling a hat out of the bag. Ask each one, "What kind of worker wears this hat?" After identifying the worker, the child does a pantomime of the worker performing the job. Include some discussion about how dads can be nurses and moms can be construction workers.

HAVE YOU SEEN MY FATHER OR MOTHER?

The children form a circle. One child stands in the center of the circle with eyes closed or hidden as you silently point to another child. Then the child in the center looks up and asks, "Have you seen my father (or mother)?" The others say in a chorus, "Yes, we have seen your father!" Then they proceed to describe the child you had pointed to earlier, taking turns to say things like, "He's wearing red overalls" or "He has brown hair."

When the child in the center has identified the father, the father performs some movement appropriate to his role (hugs a child, drives a car) and all the children imitate him. Repeat the game until everybody has had a turn being a parent.

READING THE NEWSPAPER

The children pretend to be moms and dads reading the newspaper. They shake the paper—what sound does it make? Can they rustle their bodies like a newspaper?

Have the children choose partners. One child is the newsboy or newsgirl who tosses the paper to the other child, who pretends to be mom or dad catching the paper. Have the children all pretend to be newspaper blowing in the wind. Give them real pages of the paper to crumple into a ball. Let them roll their balls, toss them to partners, blow them across the floor.

When you say that mom and dad are through reading the paper and are going to bed, the children lie down on the floor and rest.

MOTHER, MAY I?

The children line up on one side of a room or yard. The "Mother" (designate a child) stands on the opposite side and calls upon the first child in line to take a certain kind of step or jump (giant step, baby step, scissor step, hop, skip, etc.). That child must ask, "Mother, may I?" and wait until Mother answers, "Yes, you may." Then the child can take the step.

Mother continues to tell each child in turn what kind of step to take. The first child to reach and tag the Mother plays the Mother in the next round. Make sure each child has a turn being the Mother (or Father). You may have to have a pair of children be Mother and Father at the same time.

BOOKS TO READ ALOUD

Alda, Arlene. *Matthew and His Dad.* Simon and Schuster, 1983.
_____ . *Sonya's Mommy Works.* Simon and Schuster, 1982.
Asche, Frank. *Goodnight Horsey.* Prentice-Hall, 1981.
Blaine, Marge. *The Terrible Thing That Happened at Our House.* Scholastic, 1975.
Brownstone, Cecily. *All Kinds of Mothers.* David McKay, 1969.
Carton, Lonnie. *Daddies.* Random House, 1963.
Eastman, P. D. *Are You My Mother?* Random House, 1960.
Fisher, Aileen. *My Mother and I.* Crowell, 1967.
Kindred, Wendy. *Ida's Idea.* McGraw Hill, 1972.
Lasker, Joe. *Mothers Can Do Anything.* Albert Whitman, 1972.
MacLachlan, Patricia. *Mama One, Mama Two.* Harper and Row, 1982.
Merriam, Eve and Beni Montresor. *Mommies at Work.* Knopf, 1961.

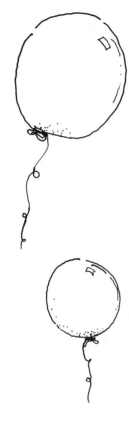

Parsons, Ellen. *Rainy Day Together*. Harper and Row, 1971.

Smith, Lucia B. *My Mom Got a Job*. Holt, Rinehart and Winston, 1979.

Stecher, Miriam B. *Daddy and Ben Together*. Lothrop, Lee and Shepard, 1981.

Stewart, Robert. *The Daddy Book*. McGraw Hill, 1972.

Titherington, Jeanne. *Big World, Small World*. Greenwillow, 1985.

Wandra, Mark. *My Daddy Is a Nurse*. Addison-Wesley, 1981.

Wells, Rosemary. *Hazel's Magic Mother*. Dial, 1985.

Families Are Different:

Adams, Florence. *Mushy Eggs*. Putnam, 1973.

Bagwell, E. and Meeks, E. *Families Live Together*. Follett, 1969.

Boegehold, Betty. *Daddy Doesn't Live Here Anymore*. Western, 1985.

Caines, Jeanette. *Daddy*. Harper and Row, 1977.

Cervante, Alex. *Saturday with Daddy*. Dandelion, 1982.

Dragonwagon, Crescent. *Always, Always*. Macmillan, 1984.

Kindred, Wendy. *Lucky Wilma*. Dial, 1973.

Lisker, Sonia O. *Two Special Cards*. Harcourt, 1976.

Noble, June. *Where Do I Fit In?* Holt, Rinehart and Winston, 1981.

Perry, Patricia and Lynch, Marietta. *Mommy and Daddy Are Divorced*. Dial, 1978.

Schuchman, Joan. *Two Places to Sleep*. Carolrhoda Books, 1979.

Seuling, Barbara. *What Kind of Family Is This?* Western, 1985.

Sonneborn, Ruth A. *Friday Night Is Papa Night*. Viking, 1970.

Stinson, Kathy. *Mom and Dad Don't Live Together Anymore*. Annick Press, 1984.

Taylor, Mark. *Families*. Allyn and Bacon, 1978.

Thomas, Ianthe. *Eliza's Daddy*. Harcourt, 1976.

Zindel, Paul. *I Love My Mother*. Harper and Row, 1976.

Zolotow, Charlotte. *A Father Like That*. Harper and Row, 1971.

BROTHERS AND SISTERS

Children experience a whole range of emotions toward their younger and older brothers and sisters, but underlying all their mixed feelings is a strong sibling bond. A four-year-old may occasionally threaten to throw her baby brother out with the garbage, but she will also feel very proprietary when another child wants to play with "her baby."

Let your children explore their relationships with their brothers and sisters in their art, music, and movement activities. Remember, however, that *families are different*. Some children may be only children or have step-siblings in another household. Ask these children to think about other family members or friends with whom they have sister, or brother-like relationships. Or perhaps the child has an imaginary brother or sister.

ART ACTIVITIES

WHEN I'M ANGRY

Materials: Construction paper, marker, styrofoam meat tray, paint, toy hammers with plastic or wooden heads.
Preparation: Pour paint into the styrofoam tray.
Activity: Discuss with the children situations in which they fought with their brothers or sisters. Talk about how angry they felt—angry enough to pound or hit. Give them play hammers for printing, not pounding. The children dip the hammer heads in paint and make prints on paper.

Families are different: Suggest that children without brothers or sisters get just as angry at other family members or friends.

SISTERS OR BROTHERS COLLAGE

Materials: Construction paper, magazines, catalogs, scissors, glue.
Activity: Children look through magazines and cut out pictures of boys and girls. They glue these brothers and sisters on paper to make a collage.

MY BABY'S CRADLE

Materials: Oats or cornmeal carton with lid, glue, scissors, paint, paintbrush, shellac, pieces of cotton.
Preparation: Cut a section out of the carton as shown. Cut two semi-circles out of the cutout section before discarding it.

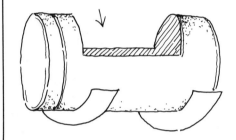

cut section from carton

glue rockers to carton

decorate and add cotton

Activity: Children glue the lids on their cartons, then glue the rockers on the bottom of the cradle. Next they paint their cradles however they like. When the paint is dry, shellac the cradles to protect them. Give the children wads of cotton to place in the cradle as a mattress. A small baby doll will find the cradle a comfortable bed.

Families are different: Children who don't have baby brothers or sisters will nevertheless enjoy art projects about babies. After all, they were once babies themselves!

BABY'S PLAYPEN

Materials: Styrofoam block (ask a TV or appliance store for styrofoam packaging), four sticks or bamboo skewers, mesh from an onion bag or embroidery netting, construction paper, scissors.

Preparation: Trim the styrofoam to a square if necessary. Cut a length of netting to fit around the styrofoam base. It should be about four inches wide.

Activity: Children stick the skewers or sticks into the corners of the styrofoam base so they stand about four inches high. They wrap the netting around the sticks, removing the sticks and weaving them through the netting at that point if they can, or gluing the netting in place. Give the children construction paper so they can draw and cut out a baby to put in the playpen. Or they might want to put in a small doll, such as a Fisher-Price person.

OUR BABY CRAWLS

Materials: Construction paper, scissors, black marker, two pipe cleaners, empty thread spool, glue.

Preparation: Cut out a paper circle two inches in diameter.

Activity: Children twist two pipe cleaners together—the middle of one around the middle of the other. They poke the pipe cleaners through the spool, then bend down the ends to form the baby's bent arms and legs. Next the children draw faces on their paper circles. Help them glue the face above the arms on the spool.

SISTER'S PONYTAIL

Materials: Magazine picture of girl with pigtails or a ponytail, building block, aluminum foil, rubber bands, construction paper, styrofoam meat tray, paint.

Preparation: Pour paint into the styrofoam tray.

Activity: Children wrap their blocks in foil and stretch several rubber bands around them. They dip the blocks in paint and stamp on paper so the rubber bands make a printed design.

Families are different: No sister? Perhaps the child wears her own hair in pigtails or a ponytail, or has a friend or classmate who does.

MUSIC AND MOVEMENT ACTIVITIES

IN MY BROTHER'S OR SISTER'S SHOES

Collect a bagful of shoes that the children's brothers and sisters would use for specific activities, for example, ballet or tap dancing shoes, boots, beach thongs, bedroom slippers, sneakers, dress shoes, booties, and baby shoes. The children take turns pulling a shoe out of the bag, telling what kind of shoe it is and who in the family would wear it. Then all the children pretend to be that family member and do a pantomime of what the person would do in the shoe. The children might crawl for a bootie, dance on their toes for a ballet shoe, pretend to swim for the beach thong, and so on.

Families are different: Children without their own brothers or sisters will be just as interested in exploring what someone else's brothers or sisters do. Or you can drop the sibling emphasis altogether and ask, "What would a child do in these shoes?"

SONG: "Are You Sleeping?"

Sing this variation of "Frere Jacques," substituting the names of the children's brothers and sisters.

> Are you sleeping?
> Are you sleeping?
> Sister Katie? Sister Katie?
> I would like to play with you
> I would like to play with you
> Please wake up.
> Please wake up.

GROWING BABIES

The children pretend they are baby brothers or sisters and move accordingly as you describe their age and activities. As eight-month-olds, they crawl around the floor. On their first birthday, the babies take their first wobbly steps, then fall down. Soon the babies walk without falling, then they run, and before long they can jump on two feet. Now the babies are three-year-olds (or four) who can walk, run, hop on one foot as well as two, and gallop. And now—our big grown-up boy (or girl) is five years old and *not* a baby anymore! The children skip around the room to show they're all grown up.

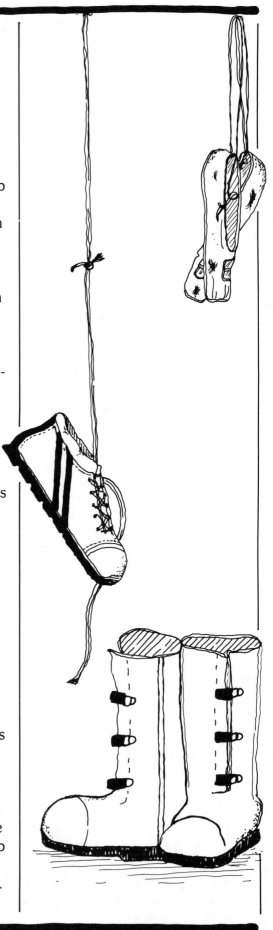

ROCKING CRADLES

To make cradles with their bodies, the children lie on the floor, draw their knees to their chests and clasp their hands around them. They rock (up and down) on their bottoms and lower backs as they sing "Rockabye Baby."

POWDER THE BABY

The children pretend to be babies after a bath. Narrate as the children act out your suggestions: "Mommy dries you and sprinkles baby powder on you. She rubs it on your shoulders, arms, stomach, bottom, feet. (*Rub the different body parts.*) Oh, no! The powder is sprinkling on the floor! (*Children shake their whole bodies.*) Shake your head, shoulders, arms, hands, feet. What a mess!"

BOOKS TO READ ALOUD

Alexander, Martha. *I'll Be the Horse If You'll Play with Me.* Dial, 1975.

——————— . *Nobody Asked Me If I Wanted a Baby Sister.* Dial, 1971.

Arnstein, Helene S. *Billy and Our New Baby.* Behavioral Publications, 1973.

Berenstain, Jan and Stan. *The Berenstain Bears' New Baby.* Random House, 1974.

——————— . *The Berenstain Bears Get in a Fight.* Random House, 1982.

Berger, Terry. *A New Baby.* Raintree, 1974.

——————— . *Big Sister, Little Brother.* Children's Press, 1974.

Byars, Betsy. *Go and Hush the Baby.* Viking, 1971.

de Poix, Carol. *Jo, Flo, and Yolanda.* Lollipop Power, 1973.

Edelman, Elaine. *I Love My Baby Sister.* Puffin Books, 1984.

Fleisher, Robbin. *Quilts in the Attic.* Macmillan, 1978.

Fujikawa, Gyo. *Me Too!* Grosset and Dunlap, 1982.

Hazen, Barbara S. *Why Couldn't I Be an Only Kid Like You, Wigger?* Atheneum, 1975.

Hill, Elizabeth S. *Evan's Corner.* Holt, Rinehart and Winston, 1967.

Hoban, Russell. *A Baby Sister for Frances.* Harper and Row, 1964.

Holland, Vicki. *We Are Having a Baby.* Scribner's, 1972.

Keats, Ezra J. *Peter's Chair.* Harper and Row, 1967.

Klein, Norma. *Girls Can Be Anything.* Dutton, 1973.

Lasker, Joe. *He's My Brother.* Albert Whitman, 1974.

Merriam, Eve. *Boys and Girls, Girls and Boys.* Holt, Rinehart and Winston, 1972.

Schick, Eleanor. *Peggy's New Brother.* Macmillan, 1970.

Scott, Ann H. *On Mother's Lap.* McGraw Hill, 1972.

Seuling, Barbara. *The Triplets.* Houghton Mifflin, 1980.

Vigna, Judith. *Couldn't We Have a Turtle Instead?* Albert Whitman, 1975.

Weiss, Nicki. *Chuckie.* Greenwillow, 1982.

Wells, Rosemary. *Noisy Nora.* Dial, 1973.

Zolotow, Charlotte. *Big Sister and Little Sister.* Harper and Row, 1976.

——————— . *Do You Know What I'll Do?* Harper and Row, 1958.

GRANDPARENTS

Grandparents hold a special place in a child's heart. Who else but a grandparent offers such unconditional love? Only a parent, and in some households grandparents play that role as well.

Grandparents are different: some are middle-aged, others are quite old; some are active and healthy, others are confined to a wheelchair or bed; some are alert and lively, others' minds are fading. While one child enjoys a grandparent, another may be coping with a grandparent's death or debilitation.

Be sensitive to the very different experiences your children may be having with their grandparents. Whenever necessary, follow suggestions for adapting or reinterpreting an activity to make it appropriate for a child's special circumstances.

ART ACTIVITIES

GRAM OR GRAMP WALKS WITH WHEELS

Materials: Three styrofoam cups, scissors, brass paper fasteners, oaktag, two pipe cleaners.
Preparation: Cut out the bottoms of two styrofoam cups for wheels.
Activity: Children cut an inch off the top of the third cup all around, then cut and fold out a square opening for a seat. Help them attach a wheel on each side of the seat with brass fasteners. Next they cut a small strip of oaktag as wide as the opening for the seat. They fold the strip down at the top and up at the bottom to form a foot rest, then glue the top inside the seat opening. Last they attach pipe cleaners as handles on the back of the wheelchair.

Families are different: Many children have young, healthy grandparents who do not use wheelchairs and may never need them. These children can attach rockers instead of wheels to the sides of the chair and make a rocking chair in which Grandma or Grandpa rocks and reads to them.

MY GRANDMA

Materials: Teflon pot or copper pot scrubber, pipe cleaners, styrofoam ball 1½ inches in diameter, yarn, felt scraps, glue.

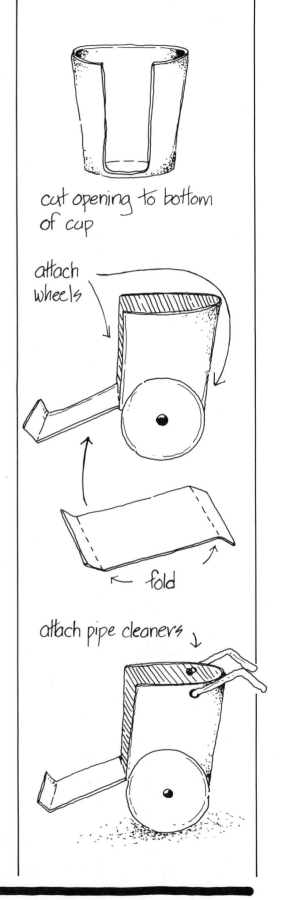

cut opening to bottom of cup

attach wheels

← fold

attach pipe cleaners ↓

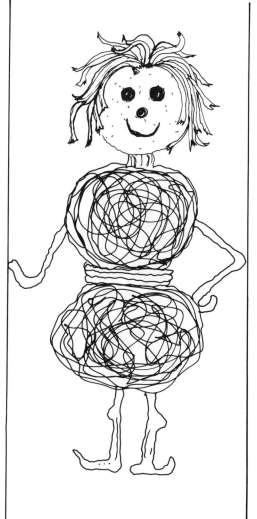

Activity: Children wrap a pipe cleaner around the middle of the pot scrubber for Grandma's trunk. They bend another pipe cleaner in half, poke both ends into the styrofoam ball to form a neck and head, then attach the head to the trunk by weaving the pipe cleaner neck through the pot scrubber. They also weave in pipe cleaner arms and legs. Last, the children make face features, hands and shoes from felt scraps, hair from yarn, and glue all these in place. *Note: Four- and five-year-olds can do this activity. Most three-year-olds don't have the fine motor skills to weave pipe cleaners.*

EYEGLASSES FOR GRANDMA OR GRANDPA

Materials: Egg carton, scissors, pipe cleaners, paint, paintbrush.

Preparation: Cut out two egg carton sections, keeping them attached. Cut out eyeholes. Poke a small hole on each side of the glasses with a scissors.

Activity: Children paint their eyeglasses. When the paint dries, they attach pipe cleaner frames through the small holes on either side of the glasses.

Families are different: Even if Grandma and Grandpa don't wear eyeglasses, they might wear sunglasses.

GRANDPARENTS' DAY PAINTING

Materials: White construction paper, watercolor paint, paintbrush, container of water, empty pasta box (the kind with a cellophane window), scissors, yarn, glue.

Preparation: Cut out the cellophane window in the pasta box, leaving a narrow border all around. Trace the window cutout on both a piece of cardboard (the back panel of the pasta box is fine) and a piece of paper, and cut those pieces out as well.

Activity: Children paint a picture on the paper cutout with watercolor paints. When the paint dries, they glue the picture to the plain cardboard backing. Staple a piece of yarn on each side on top of the backing for a hanger, then have the children glue the frame (the window) on top of the picture.

GRANDPA'S TIE-DYE NECKTIE

Materials: Cotton fabric, scissors, rubber bands, large pan or bucket, commercial dye, large spoon, water, newspapers.

Preparation: Cut off a long strip of fabric for a necktie. Mix the dye with water in the pan according to the directions on the package. Spread a lot of newspaper around the work area.

Activity: Children soak their tie in cold water for a few minutes, then wring out the water. They wind rubber bands around different sections of the tie, or twist and tie the different sections. Then they lower the tie into the dye with a large spoon. After dyeing the tie, they rinse it thoroughly in cold water, remove the rubber bands or untwist the tie, and rinse again. If you have more than one color dye, they can repeat the procedure with another color. Let Grandpa's tie dry flat or hang dry.

LOCKET FOR MY GRANDMA

Materials: Red construction paper, scissors, stapler, child's photo, glue, ziti noodles, colored markers, yarn.
Preparation: Fold the red paper and cut out a double heart hinged on one side. Cut out a narrow strip of paper. Open the heart-shaped locket. Make the ends of the paper strip meet, then staple them to the inside of the locket.
Activity: Children cut out a picture of themselves from a photo and glue the cutout on the inside of the locket. Next they decorate the ziti noodles with colored markers. They string half the ziti beads onto a piece of yarn, then the locket, then the rest of the beads.

MUSIC AND MOVEMENT ACTIVITIES

SONG: "Grandma and Grandpa Have Come to Visit Me"

Sing this song to the tune of "The Itsy Bitsy Spider."

> Grandma and Grandpa have come to visit me,
> I am the one that they have come to see.
> They bring a surprise, they play with me, and then
> Grandma and Grandpa must go back home again.
> Goodbye! (*Children blow kisses.*)

> *Families are different*: You may instead want to sing "My Grandma Carol. . . (each child names a grandparent)" or "My Uncle Bob. . . (each child names a relative)" for those children who have only one or no living grandparent.

HOW GRANDMAS AND GRANDPAS WALK

The children walk and move the different ways they see their grandparents and other old people do it. They walk slowly, briskly, with a cane, in a wheelchair, jog, and so on.

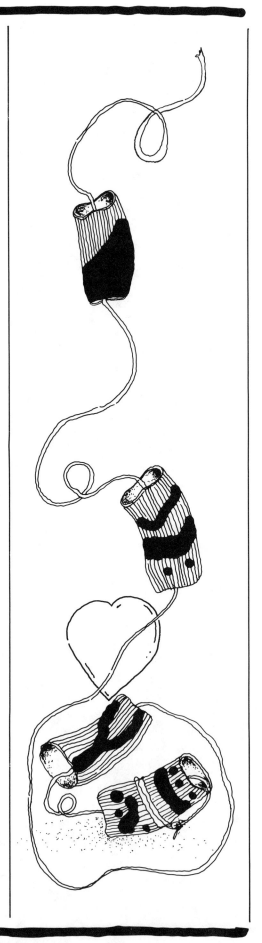

FOLLOW GRANDMA, FOLLOW GRANDPA

Play follow the leader. The leader pretends to be Grandma or Grandpa and performs an action that a grandparent might do. The other children imitate. For example, the grandparents might pretend to bake cookies, ride a bike, knit a sweater, read a book, take a walk, go shopping, garden, or hug their grandchildren.

PRESENTS FROM GRANDMA AND GRANDPA

Wrap a box and its lid separately in wrapping paper. Open the box a little, peek inside, and ask, ''Can you guess what's inside this box? Grandma and Grandpa brought you a present!'' The children take turns performing a pantomime showing the contents of the box. Encourage them to disregard the size and shape of the box and to imagine whatever kind of gift they themselves might want to receive, or actually have received, from their grandparents.

BOOKS TO READ ALOUD

Buckley, Helen. *Grandfather and I.* Lothrop, Lee and Shepard, 1959.

———— . *Grandmother and I.* Lothrop, Lee and Shepard, 1961.

Burningham, John. *Granpa.* Crown, 1985.

de Paola, Tomie. *Now One Foot, Now the Other.* Putnam, 1973.

———— . *Nana Upstairs, Nana Downstairs.* Putnam, 1973.

Gauch, Patricia L. *Grandpa and Me.* Coward, McCann and Geoghegan, 1972.

Goldman, Susan. *Grandpa and Me Together.* Albert Whitman, 1980.

Greenfield, Eloise. *Grandma's Joy.* Putnam, 1980.

Kenworthy, Catherine. *A Visit from Grandma and Grandpa.* Western, 1982.

Lasky, Kathryn. *I Have Four Names for My Grandfather.* Little, Brown, 1976.

Moore, Elaine. *Grandma's House.* Lothrop, 1985.

Rappaport, Doreen. *But She's Still My Grandma!* Human Sciences Press, 1982.

Sonneborn, Ruth. *I Love Gram.* Viking, 1971.

Udry, Janice M. *Mary Jo's Grandmother.* Albert Whitman, 1972.

Williams, Barbara. *Kevin's Grandma.* Dutton, 1975.

Zolotow, Charlotte. *My Grandson Lew.* Harper and Row, 1974.

BABYSITTERS

In households where both parents or a single parent work out of the home, the babysitter joins that circle of important people a child considers family. The sitter may actually be family—a grandparent, for example. Or the sitter may be a housekeeper, nanny, teen-ager after school, or a person who provides daycare in a center or his or her own home.

Then again, *families are different*. For some children, a parent is always waiting at home. But even these children have occasion to spend time with a babysitter, if only for an afternoon or evening while Mom takes a class, or Mommy and Daddy go out to a movie by themselves.

ART ACTIVITIES

WATCHING TV TOGETHER

Materials: Large cardboard carton, scissors, paint, paintbrush, black poster board, brass paper fasteners.
Preparation: Cut an opening for a TV screen out of one side of the box. Cut off the opposite panel entirely. Cut two circles out of black poster board for dials.
Activity: Children paint the make-believe television. When the paint is dry, attach the dials below the screen opening with brass fasteners. The children can set the TV on a table, stand behind the screen, and perform for the babysitter.

NANNY'S ROOM

Materials: Shoebox, magazines and catalogs, scissors, glue.
Activity: Children look through magazines and catalogs for items resembling those in their live-in babysitter's room. They cut out the pictures and glue them into the shoebox room.

Families are different: Children whose babysitters don't live with the family can make their own bedroom or any other room where they spend time with sitters. They can glue in picture objects (TV, books, blocks) that show what they do with their sitters.

remove back panel and cut an opening for the screen

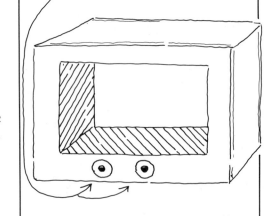

let children paint their TV's and add knobs

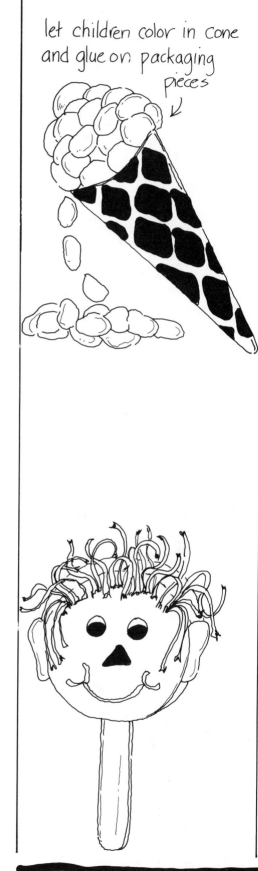

let children color in cone and glue on packaging pieces

DAYS OR NIGHTS TOGETHER

Materials: Construction paper, crayons, felt-tip pen, stapler.
Activity: Children draw a picture of something they do with their babysitter. Ask about the picture and write each child's spoken words under that child's picture. When the children have each made several drawings showing activities they do with their babysitters, staple the drawings together to make a book that the babysitter and the child can read together.

SHARING A TREAT

Materials: White construction paper, scissors, brown crayon, styrofoam packaging pieces, glue, red button.
Preparation: Cut an ice cream cone out of construction paper or make a pattern for the children to trace and cut out themselves.
Activity: Children color in the cone. They glue the styrofoam packing pieces on the scoop of ice cream, and the button on top for a cherry.

READING BOOKS TOGETHER

Materials: Construction paper, pinking shears, styrofoam meat tray and black paint (or black stamp pad).
Preparation: Cut out a large bookmark with the pinking shears. Pour the paint into the styrofoam tray.
Activity: The children dip their thumbs in the paint and make thumbprints on their bookmarks. Suggest that the children place their bookmarks in books they like to read with their babysitters, perhaps to mark a favorite illustration.

MY BABYSITTER

Materials: Empty margarine tub, knife, tongue depressor or Popsicle stick, colored markers, felt and fabric scraps, rolling plastic eyeballs (available at crafts stores), yarn or cotton balls, pipe cleaners.
Preparation: Slit the side of the margarine tub with a knife and push in the tongue depressor.
Activity: Children make the face of their babysitter by gluing on the plastic eyeballs, a pipe cleaner mouth, felt nose and ears, yarn or cotton hair (and mustache or beard, if appropriate).

MUSIC AND MOVEMENT ACTIVITIES

THINGS WE DO TOGETHER

The children act out some of the things they do with their babysitters. Some possibilities include cook dinner, wash dishes, take a walk, go shopping, read a book, watch TV, play games, pick up a brother or sister.

BAG FULL OF TOYS

Show the children a large tote bag and tell them it is full of toys they are bringing to their babysitter's house (or that the babysitter is bringing to the child's house). The children take turns pulling an imaginary toy out of the bag and doing a pantomime to help the others guess what they have pulled out. If the children need some suggestions, the toys might include a deck of cards, a ball and jacks, a truck, a doll, a book, building blocks.

HELPING A HOUSEKEEPER

The children use hoops to pretend they are helping a housekeeper who cares for them to do cleaning chores.

>Dust the furniture. (*Children swivel their hips to move hoops around their waists.*)
>Vacuum the floor. (*Children push hoops along the floor in front of them.*)
>Pick up the clothes. (*Children put hoops on the floor, then pick them up, repeating several times.*)
>Wash the windows. (*Children hold hoops above their heads and move them back and forth.*)
>Make the bed. (*Children pretend to tuck in sheets around hoops on the floor.*)

BOOKS TO READ ALOUD

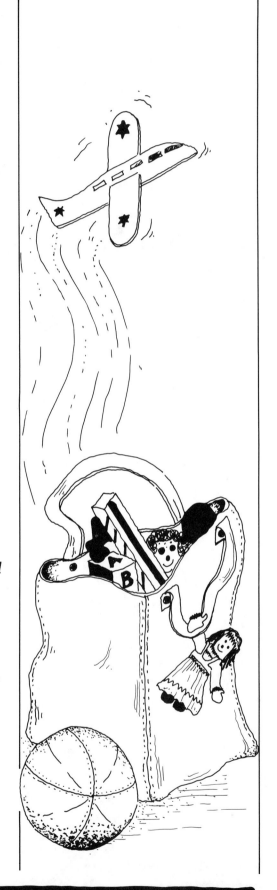

Adams, Florence. *Mushy Eggs.* Putnam, 1973.
Alda, Arlene. *Sonya's Mommy Works.* Simon and Schuster, 1982.
Berenstain, Stan and Jan. *The Berenstain Bears and the Sitter.* Random House, 1981.
Chalmers, Mary. *Be Good, Harry.* Harper and Row, 1967.
Greenberg, Barbara. *The Bravest Babysitter.* Dial, 1978.
Harris, Robie H. *Don't Forget to Come Back.* Knopf, 1978.
Hughes, Shirley. *George the Babysitter.* Prentice-Hall, 1975.
——————. *An Evening at Alfie's.* Lothrop, Lee and Shepard, 1984.
Kenworthy, Catherine. *A Visit from Grandma and Grandpa.* Western, 1982.
Steptoe, John. *Stevie.* Harper and Row, 1969.
Wells, Rosemary. *Stanley and Rhoda.* Dial, 1978.

Chapter Two:

Children Have Fun

FRIENDS

Young children feel strongly about their friends, whether they're young, old, or pretend. They look forward to seeing their playmates every day, and preoccupy themselves wondering what their friends are up to when they are not in school or playing together. The prospect of having a friend over for lunch will brighten the gloomiest of days; even a short visit promises to be fun.

ART ACTIVITIES

HANDS IN FRIENDSHIP

Materials: Construction paper, styrofoam meat tray, paint.
Preparation: Pour the paint into the styrofoam tray.
Activity: Friends make their handprints together on construction paper. Provide enough paper so that each child can keep a handprint picture.

COLOR FRIENDS

Materials: Construction paper, primary color paints, spoons.
Preparation: This activity should follow a reading of the book *Little Blue and Little Yellow* (listed in the bibliography). Talk about how colors form friendships.
Activity: Children fold a piece of construction paper in half. They spoon blue and yellow paint on the paper, then refold and press down on the paper. The colors will bleed together and produce a symmetrical design of blue, yellow, and green. Repeat the activity using red and blue together to make purple, and red and yellow together to make orange.

STUFFED ANIMAL FRIEND

Materials: Brown wrapping paper or grocery bag, scissors, hole punch, yarn, colored markers, newspaper.
Preparation: Cut an animal shape—teddy bear, dog, cat, bunny—out of the brown paper. Use that shape as a pattern to cut out another (or fold the paper and cut out two at a time). Put one shape on top of the other and punch holes all around the edges. Shred newspaper into thin strips. Tape around one end of the yarn and knot the other through one of the holes in the shape.
Activity: Children sew around the edges of their animals, stopping a few holes before the end to stuff them with newspaper strips. Then they finish sewing.

stuff with shredded newspaper before sewing is complete

glue bottle cap
pictures in windows

cut out photos and
glue inside bottle caps

FRIENDSHIP BOOK

Materials: Construction paper, crayons, stapler.
Activity: Children draw several self-portraits to give to their friends. When the children have collected pictures from all their friends, help them assemble them in a friendship book. Put a construction paper cover on top of the pictures and staple them together along the top or side. Write My Friendship Book across each cover, then let the children decorate their own covers.

FRIENDSHIP HOUSE

Materials: Oaktag, scissors, photographs of friends, bottle caps (the kind you have to remove with a bottle opener), glue.
Preparation: Make a pattern for a large house out of oaktag. Cut out the faces of friends from the photos so they will fit inside the bottle caps.
Activity: Children trace the house pattern on colored construction paper and cut it out. Help the children cut out many windows and a door. Have them glue the house onto a piece of oaktag. Next they glue the photos inside the bottle caps, then glue each cap in a window or door of the house. The children can make one house together or they can make their own houses.

FRIENDS SHARING

Materials: Brown wrapping paper, styrofoam meat tray, paint, raw vegetables for printing.
Preparation: Tear off a large piece of paper. Pour the paint into the styrofoam tray.
Activity: Each child selects a vegetable to share with friends. Cut the vegetable into pieces so each child can have a piece. Friends dip their vegetables into the paint and make prints on the paper. After the paint dries, display the vegetable mural on a wall.

MUSIC AND MOVEMENT ACTIVITIES

SONG: "When We See Our Friends in the Morning"

Make up a simple tune and sing this song. Repeat until you have sung each child's name.

> When we see Jeff in the morning
> We always say, "Good day!"
> When we see Jeff in the morning
> We always say, "Good day!"
> "Hello, hello, hello, hello!"
> That is what we say, we say.
> "Hello, hello, hello, hello!"
> That is what we say.

MIRROR A FRIEND

The children sit in a circle. One child looks at a friend and observes the way the other child is sitting. Count to three out loud. The child sits like the friend. Count to three again as the child changes position. Continue to play, giving each child a chance to mirror the positions of several other children in the circle.

FRIENDLY EFFORT

Five or six children get down on all fours and form a line. They crawl under a sheet or blanket and pretend to be one long animal or machine (ask them to tell you what they are pretending to be). The friends have to work together to move forward or backward and still keep their covered form.

SONG: "The More We Get Together"

Sing this old favorite as your group sits in a close circle holding hands and swaying from side to side. Sing as many additional verses as necessary to mention all the friends' names.

> The more we get together, together, together
> The more we get together, the happier we'll be.
> 'Cause your friends are my friends,
> And my friends are your friends.
> The more we get together, the happier we'll be.
> Here's Joanie and Peter and Mark and Lisa
> The more we get together, the happier we'll be.

"move sideways"

"move backwards"

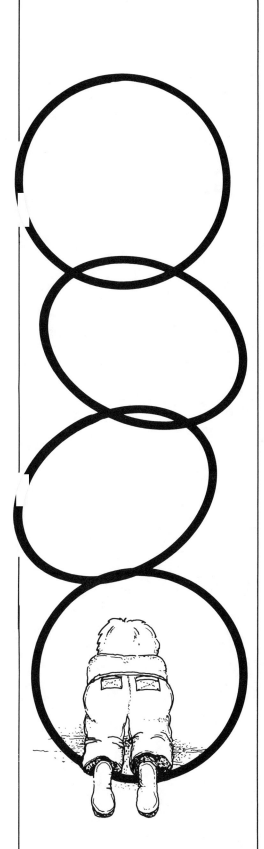

RING OF FRIENDSHIP

Place a hoop on the floor. The children form a line. As you name the movement, the children one after the other walk, jump, hop, or crawl through the ring of friendship. Ask one child to put the ring around a friend, then that child puts the ring around another friend, and so on until all the children have worn the ring.

FRIENDSHIP HEART

The children lie down on the floor and position their bodies in such a way that they form the shape of a heart. Stand on a chair and take a photograph of the friendship heart. Make a print for each child as a friendship souvenir.

BOOKS TO READ ALOUD

Aliki. *We Are Best Friends*. William Morrow, 1972.
Brown, Marcia. *Stone Soup, An Old Tale*. Scribner's, 1947.
Brown, Myra B. *Best Friends*. Golden Gate, 1967.
Carle, Eric. *Do You Want to Be My Friend?* Crowell, 1971.
Cohen, Miriam. *Will I Have a Friend?* Macmillan, 1967.
_____ . *Best Friends*. Macmillan, 1971.
Ets, Marie H. *Play with Me*. Viking, 1955.
Freeman, Don. *Corduroy*. Viking, 1968.
Fujikawa, Gyo. *Welcome Is a Wonderful Word*. Grosset and Dunlap, 1980.
Heine, Helme. *Friends*. Atheneum, 1982.
Hoban, Russell. *Best Friends for Frances*. Harper and Row, 1969.
Ichikawa, S. *Friends*. Parent's Magazine Press, 1975.
Lionni, Leo. *Little Blue, Little Yellow*. Astor-Honor, 1969.
Lobel, Arnold. *Frog and Toad Are Friends*. Harper and Row, 1970.
Mannheim, Grete. *The Two Friends*. Knopf, 1968.
Mayer, Mercer. *A Boy, a Dog, and a Frog*. Dial, 1967.
_____ . *A Boy, a Dog, and a Friend*. Dial, 1971.
Tolstoi, Alexei. *The Great Big Enormous Turnip*. Franklyn Watts, 1969.
Udry, Janice. *Let's Be Enemies*. Harper and Row, 1969.
Wells, Rosemary. *Timothy Goes to School*. Dial, 1981.
Zolotow, Charlotte. *Hold My Hand*. Harper and Row, 1972.

PARTIES

Every child's birthday deserves a special celebration. Children can help make their own party decorations, favors, and treats—some beforehand, some as part of the festivities. Here's a unit full of party ideas and games.

ART ACTIVITIES

A CANDLE FOR EVERYONE

Materials: Styrofoam egg carton or half-pint milk carton, candle wick (available at crafts stores), Gulf Wax or parafin, broken crayons, empty coffee can, saucepan, oven or hot plate.

Preparation: Cut and place candle wick in each section of the egg carton or in the half-pint carton. (If you're using a half-pint carton, tie a pencil to the wick and rest it on top of the carton as shown.)

Activity: Children decide what color they want their candles to be. Place the color crayon and some wax in the coffee can. Fill the saucepan halfway with water. Put the coffee can in the saucepan and heat until the wax melts, then pour the wax into the egg carton section or half-pint carton. Let the wax harden overnight, then help the children tear away the carton. Light the birthday candles!

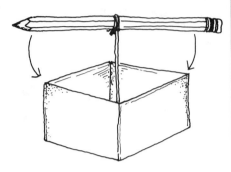

rest pencil on carton

add color crayon and wax

WRAPPING PAPER

Materials: White tissue paper, scissors, different colors of food coloring, medicine droppers (unnecessary if the food coloring containers are squeeze bottles), small pieces of sponge, newspapers.

Preparation: Fold a large sheet of tissue paper in half and half again, until you have a small square.

Activity: Children squeeze drops of food coloring on the tissue paper, blot with a piece of sponge to make the colors bleed, then unfold the papers and lay them on newspaper to dry.

GOODY BAGS

Materials: White bakery or lunch-size paper bags, colored markers.

Activity: Children decorate their own party favor bags with colored markers. If they like, they can draw pictures along the party theme.

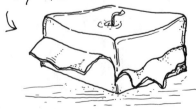

let the wax harden overnight, then tear away the carton

tape toilet tubes
to balloon

leave a small opening
for stuffing

PARTY PINATAS

Materials: Large balloon, toilet paper tubes, tape, wallpaper paste or liquid starch and glue, tissue paper or strips of newspaper, paint, paintbrushes, shellac, small prizes and goodies, materials for decorating (feathers, sequins, felt scraps, bows), wire, stick.

Preparation: Inflate the large balloon. Tape on toilet tube rolls to make legs, ears, a tail, or other animal parts. Make a papier mache paste by mixing wallpaper paste into warm water until you have a thin, creamy mixture, or mix liquid starch and white glue until you reach the same consistency.

Activity: Children cover the creature with papier mache, layers of newspaper strips, or tissue paper soaked in the paste, leaving a small opening in the bottom. Let the construction dry thoroughly over a day or two. Have the children paint the pinata bright colors, then shellac over their work. When the shellac dries, they can glue on decorations—feathers, felt face features, sequins, glitter, bows. Pop the balloon through the opening and fasten a piece of wire to the top of the animal. Help the children pack the pinata with toys and goodies, then tape the hole closed. To play, hang the pinata and have the children take turns beating it with a stick until the toys and goodies spill out.

NOISY NOISEMAKERS

Materials: Two white paper bowls, rice or dried beans, stapler, colored tissue paper, glue.

Preparation: Staple the bowls together around the rims, leaving an opening.

Activity: Children fill the bowl shaker with rice or beans. Staple closed the opening. Now the children can decorate their noisemakers by gluing on small pieces of colored tissue paper.

DECORATE A CUPCAKE

Materials: Cupcakes, frosting (canned or homemade), knife, tube of gel for writing on cakes, small candies, licorice strings, miniature marshmallows.

Preparation: Bake a cupcake for each child attending the party.

Activity: Children ice their own cupcakes, then use writing tubes, candies, and such to turn their cupcakes into creatures. For example, they can sqeeze out gel to draw features, or press in small candy eyes, noses, and mouths. Snips of licorice strings can stick out as hair, a beard, quills, or antennae.

STRING-ALONG STREAMERS

Materials: String or colored yarn, colored construction paper, scissors, glue.

Preparation: Cut string or yarn into long lengths—as long as six feet. Knot both ends of each string to prevent unraveling. Make a pattern for cutouts along your party theme (baseballs, hearts, pumpkins, stars, flowers, bunnies, for example).

Activity: Children draw and trace their own patterns, or use yours. Have them cut out two decorations at a time so the pairs will match exactly when they are glued along the string. The space between the decorations depends on how many a child has cut out altogether to glue on the streamer.

PARTY PLACE MATS

Materials: Construction paper, colored markers, clear contact paper, scissors.

Activity: Children draw party pictures or design with markers on a piece of construction paper. Cover the front and back of each picture with clear contact paper to protect it. Show the children how to cut a fringed edge on the short sides of their place mats.

MUSIC AND MOVEMENT ACTIVITIES

WHO AM I?

Paint each child's face using cotton swabs and water-soluble face paint. Paint different characters or subjects that the children can act out—a monster (fangs), black cat (whiskers), pirate (an eye patch), Milky Way (stars). To show the Milky Way, a child might walk on tiptoe with fingers fluttering in the air like twinkling stars. To show a cat, a child might crawl about the room, stalking a pretend mouse.

STICKY CANDY

The children choose partners. First the partners pretend to eat a peppermint stick. As they lick, their hands get all sticky. The partners pretend to touch each other with sticky fingers. Their hands stick to their partners! Tell the children to pull themselves apart, move their hands, and stick together in a different position. Continue playing like this for a while, then suggest that the children wash each other's hands with an imaginary washcloth.

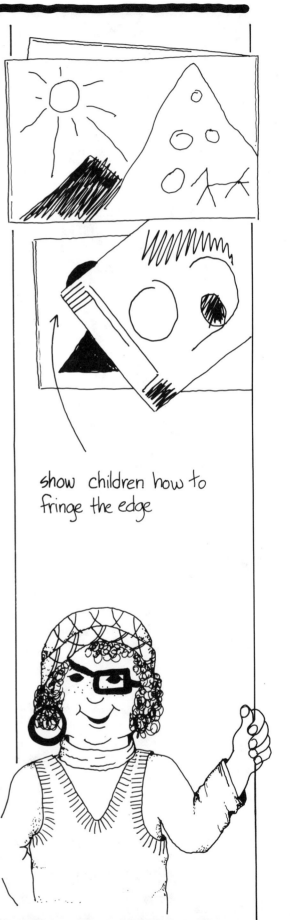

show children how to fringe the edge

CANDLES MELTING

The children pretend to be birthday candles. Light each candle (*gently tap the top of each child's head*). The children sing "Happy Birthday." As they sing, the candles slowly melt (*children very slowly fall to the floor*). By the end of the song, the children should all be lying on the floor.

PARTY BALLOONS

The children pretend to blow up balloons. Narrate as the children act out what's happening: "Blow and blow and blow! (*Children pretend to blow balloons by blowing and expanding hands.*) The balloon is so big, you need both arms around it. (*Children hold out both arms.*) Hold your balloon. (*Arms curve around.*) Now drop it. (*Arms at sides.*) Catch it! (*Arms curve around.*) And lift it. (*Lift curved arms.*) Oh, oh! The balloon blows away! Chase it! (*Children run.*) Catch it! (*Children jump with arms out.*) Oh, no! There's a tiny hole. The air is escaping! (*Children slowly fall, sputtering, to the floor.*) All the air is out of the balloon. (*Children rest on floor.*)"

THREE WISHES

The birthday child whispers a birthday wish to a second child. That child acts out the wish and the rest of the children try to guess what it is. Then the second child whispers a wish to a third child, who performs it for the others. Continue until each child has had a turn making and acting out a wish.

PEANUT HUNT

Hide small plastic bags filled with peanuts around the house, classroom, yard, or playground. The children hunt for the peanuts, then bring them to you to exchange for a different treat or prize, or the peanuts themselves can be the prize.

ROYAL BIRTHDAY PROCESSION

The birthday child is crowned king or queen and sits on a throne (a decorated chair) as each of the other children marches up and presents the royal child with a gift. After all the gifts are given, the birthday child opens them. Following the gift giving, the guests act out imaginary activities for a royal birthday celebration. For example, some children might pretend to be jugglers; others, dancing bears. The royal baker might bring out a huge cake that the royal guests pretend to eat.

BOOKS TO READ ALOUD

Bond, Felicia. *Mary Betty Lizzie McNutt's Birthday.* Crowell, 1983.

Brunhoff, Laurent de. *Babar's Birthday Surprise.* Random House, 1970.

Buckley, Helen. *The Little Boy and the Birthdays.* Lothrop, Lee and Shephard, 1965.

Carle, Eric. *Secret Birthday Message.* Harper and Row, 1968.

Cole, William. *What's Good for a Three Year Old?* Holt, Rinehart and Winston, 1974.

Fitzhugh, Louise. *I Am Four.* Delacorte, 1982.

Hoban, Russell. *A Birthday for Frances.* Harper and Row, 1968.

Hutchins, Pat. *Happy Birthday, Sam.* Greenwillow, 1978.

_____ . *The Surprise Party.* Macmillan, 1969.

Iwasaki, Chikiro. *The Birthday Wish.* McGraw Hill, 1974.

Lorian, Nicole. *A Birthday Present for Mama.* Random House, 1984.

Pomerantz, Charlotte. *The Half-Birthday Party.* Clarion Books, 1981.

Rice, Eve. *Benny Bakes a Cake.* Greenwillow, 1981.

Rockwell, Anne. *Happy Birthday to Me.* Macmillan, 1981.

Shimin, Symeon. *A Special Birthday.* McGraw Hill, 1976.

Waber, Bernard. *Lyle and the Birthday Party.* Houghton Mifflin, 1966.

Watson, Nancy D. *Tommy's Mommy's Fish.* Viking, 1971.

Wells, Rosemary. *Martha's Birthday.* Bradbury Press, 1970.

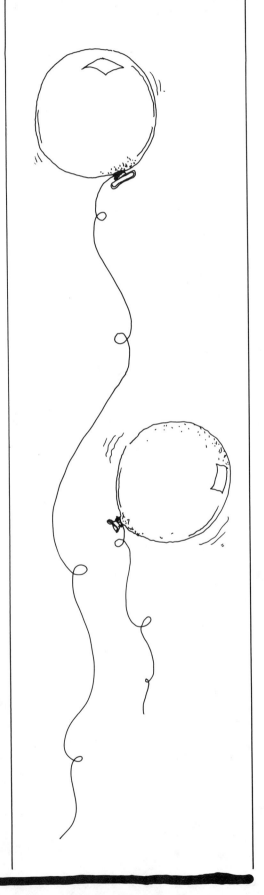

THE CIRCUS

The circus holds enchantment for children of all ages. Glittering costumes, trained animal acts, astonishing acrobatics, hilarious clowns—if your children have not yet experienced a circus, they will be awed at the mere prospect. Perhaps a one-ring circus will visit your city or town; meanwhile, your children will enjoy exploring circus themes in their artwork, music, and movement activities.

ART ACTIVITIES

TRAPEZE ARTIST

Materials: Construction paper, scissors, colored markers, glue, glitter, masking tape, wire coat hanger.

Preparation: Cut a trapeze artist out of construction paper, a figure with arms and legs extended. Or make a pattern for older children to trace and cut out.

Activity: Children draw in the facial features on their trapeze artist with colored markers and glue glitter on the costume. When the glue dries, the children tape their figures to the wire hanger so that the trapeze artist swings by the arms or upside down by the legs.

CIRCUS TRAIN ANIMAL CAR

Materials: Shoebox, scissors, poster board or cardboard, brass paper fasteners, paint, paintbrushes.

Preparation: Cut out areas of the shoebox lid to make animal cage bars. Make a circle pattern, or find a circular object for the children to trace.

Activity: Children trace the circle pattern and cut out four cardboard wheels. Attach these to the shoebox—two below the cage bars on the lid and two on the bottom of the box. Put the lid back on and stand the box on its wheels. Have the children paint their cars bright colors.

While the paint dries, the children can make elephants (see next activity) to place inside their car cages. Line up all the children's circus cars to make a long circus train.

CIRCUS ELEPHANT'S HEAD

Materials: Toilet paper tube, scissors, gray construction paper, glue, stapler, colored markers.

Preparation: Cut about 1½ inches off the toilet paper tube and discard it. Make a circle pattern that is a little larger in diameter than the height of the trimmed tube. Make another smaller circle pattern.

tape → to hanger

cut out, decorate, and hang

MARVIN MARVELOUS

Activity: Children trace three circles on gray construction paper and cut them out—one large circle for the elephant's head and two smaller circles for the ears. They also cut out a long strip of paper for the elephant's trunk. On the large circle, have them draw in eyes with a colored marker.

To assemble the elephant, the children first glue the ears on the head. Next they accordion-fold the trunk and glue one end near the bottom of the head. Staple the head onto the toilet paper tube so that it stands upright.

CIRCUS RINGS

Materials: Construction paper, styrofoam meat tray, paint, rings (canning jar rings, small embroidery hoops, jar lids, circle cookie cutters).
Preparation: Pour the paint into the styrofoam tray.
Activity: Children dip the rings in the tray of paint and make ring prints on their papers.

FIERCE FURRY LION

Materials: Brown wrapping paper, scissors, newspaper, stapler, yellow or gold yarn, felt scraps, glue, string.
Preparation: Draw a lion a yard long on the brown paper and cut out two at the same time. Staple the lions together, leaving a small opening.
Activity: The children work together to make one lion. First they stuff the lion with strips of newspaper. Help them staple the opening closed. Next they snip yarn into small pieces and glue the pieces all over both sides of the lion. On one side, they glue on facial features—eyes, nose, whiskers, and mouth—cut out of felt scraps. Suspend the lion on a long string from the ceiling.

POPCORN NECKLACE

Materials: Nylon thread, blunt needle, popped popcorn.
Preparation: Thread the needle and knot one end of the thread.
Activity: Children string popcorn to make long necklaces— long enough to fit easily over their heads. When the children are through stringing, tie the ends of the thread together to form a necklace.

CLOWNS THAT CLOWN AROUND

Materials: One large and one small paper plate, stapler, construction paper, scissors, yarn, pompon or cotton ball, buttons, glue.

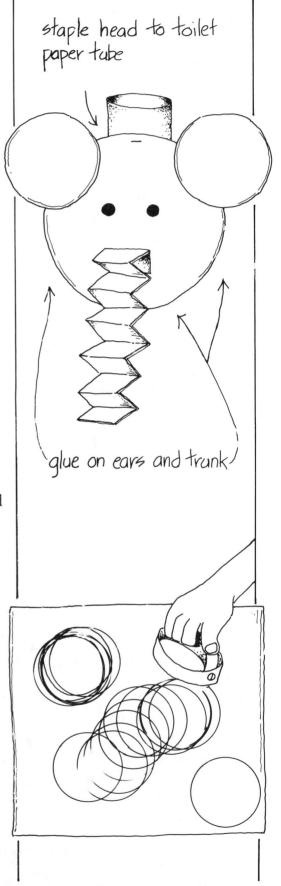

staple head to toilet paper tube

glue on ears and trunk

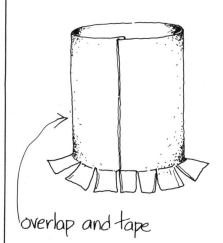

cut slits, then fold back

overlap and tape

slide brim down over crown and tape

Preparation: Staple the small plate (the head) on top of the large plate (the body).

Activity: Children cut a large triangle hat out of construction paper and decorate it with snips of yarn and a pompon. Staple the hat on the clown's head. Next the children cut long strips of paper and accordion-fold them to make arms and legs. Staple these in position on the clown's body. Last, the children glue button eyes and other yarn features—nose, mouth, hair—on the clown's face.

RINGMASTER'S HAT

Materials: Black construction paper, scissors, frozen juice can or toilet tube, paint, styrofoam tray.

Preparation: Make a pattern for a large ringmaster's hat or precut the hat out of black construction paper. Pour the paint into the styrofoam tray.

Activity: Children trace and cut a ringmaster's hat out of black construction paper. They print circus rings on their hats with a juice can or toilet tube dipped in paint.

CIRCUS ANIMAL MURAL

Materials: Brown wrapping paper, styrofoam meat trays, paints, animal cookie cutters or sponges, scissors.

Preparation: If you don't have cookie cutters, cut sponges into circus animal shapes. Pour a different-color paint into each styrofoam tray. Cut off a large piece of paper.

Activity: Children dip the cookie cutters or sponges in paint and make prints on the paper.

MUSIC AND MOVEMENT ACTIVITIES

CIRCUS ANIMAL WALK

Announce that the animals have escaped from the circus. All the cages are empty! Ask the children to move about like different circus animals. Have them lunge on all fours like lions, lumber about like bears, prance like horses, plod like heavy elephants.

ANIMAL TRAINERS

The children choose partners. One child—the animal trainer—holds out a hoop. The other child pretends to be a circus lion, bear, or dog. The circus animal follows the trainer's directions and steps in, out, around, through, over, and under the hoop. Then the children switch roles.

TIGHTROPE WALKER

Place masking tape across the floor or use a balance beam. The children pretend to be tightrope walkers. With their arms outstretched for balance, they walk on the tape or the beam forwards, backwards, and sideways.

CLOWN CAPERS

Your little clowns perform their own acts and antics. A few clowns might pretend to wear roller skates and fall down. A couple of clowns with empty spray bottles can pretend to spray water on each other. Several other clowns can pretend to have a pillow fight by throwing beanbags to each other.

THE BIG TENT

The children all take hold of a parachute or large sheet and lift it above their heads like a tent. Designate each child as a different circus animal or performer, such as an acrobat, a dancing horse, and a lion tamer. When you call out a character, that child performs under the tent while the rest of the group holds up the tent and watches.

BOOKS TO READ ALOUD

Boase, Wendy. *The Circus.* Random House, 1984.
Bridwell, Norman. *Clifford at the Circus.* Scholastic, 1977.
De Regniers, Beatrice S. *Circus.* Viking, 1966.
Du Bois, William P. *Bear Circus.* Viking, 1971.
Freeman, Don. *Bearymore.* Viking, 1976.
Hale, Irena. *Donkey's Dreadful Day.* Atheneum, 1972.
Harmen, Michael. *The Circus.* Children's Press, 1981.
Petersham, Maud. *Circus Baby.* Macmillan, 1950.
Rey, Margaret and H. A. *Curious George Goes to the Circus.* Houghton Mifflin, 1984.
Wildsmith, Brian. *Circus.* Franklin Watts, 1970.

CAMPING

Come summer, many children look forward to special family excursions. Camping—whether in a cabin, tent, or camper vehicle—is often part of a road trip or a trip to the shore, the mountains, or a lake. Some young children go to day camp, but even those who have no camping experience enjoy this outdoor adventure vicariously through books, and their own make-believe.

ART ACTIVITIES

TRAIL SNACKS

Materials: Lunch bag, magazines, scissors, glue.
Activity: Children look through magazines for pictures of snack foods, such as raisins or granola bars, to take along on an overnight camping trip or a day hike. They cut out the pictures and paste them on a lunch bag.

HIKING IN THE MOUNTAINS

Materials: Colored construction paper, cotton balls, glue.
Activity: Children use their fine motor skills to tear brown construction paper into jagged mountain shapes. They glue the mountains on a blue background and add other torn shapes—a shimmering yellow sun, puffy white clouds.

SLEEPING BAGS

Materials: Construction paper, stapler, stickers or precut shapes, scissors, glue.
Preparation: If you don't have stickers, precut flowers, teddy bears, hearts, and other shapes out of construction paper.
Activity: Help each child staple two pieces of construction paper together along three sides, leaving open one short end. The children decorate their sleeping bags with stickers of their favorite cartoon characters or things, or paste on precut shapes.

CABIN BY THE LAKE

Materials: Empty food box (cereal, crackers, pancake mix), construction paper, glue, scissors, Popsicle sticks.
Preparation: Glue the box closed and cover it with construction paper. Cut out windows and a door.
Activity: Children make a camp cabin by gluing Popsicle sticks all around the box.

CAMPING TENT

Materials: Box with square ends (as small as a shoebox or as large as a refrigerator box), utility knife or scissors, masking tape or heavy-duty stapler, colored markers or crayons.

Preparation: Cut off the square ends of the box. Cut along one fold to open the box so that the four side panels lie flat.

Activity: Show the children how to fold the cardboard to form a pyramid (A-frame tent) and tape or staple in place. (Fold down the middle of the four-panel piece, then fold in both end panels so they overlap.) The children can decorate their tents with crayons or colored markers. *Note: A group of children can help you construct a life-size tent out of a refrigerator or other large appliance box. Then they can paint murals on the inside and outside walls, or just lots of small drawings with crayons or markers. Use the tent for creative play.*

ROWBOATS

Materials: Empty dish detergent bottle, scissors, paint and paintbrush, Popsicle sticks, scraps of sponge, glue.

Preparation: Leaving the top on the detergent bottle, cut a wide oval out of the side. Make a slit on either side below the cutout area to fit in the oars.

Activity: Children paint their rowboats. Then they insert Popsicle sticks for oars and glue down pieces of sponge to make comfortable seats inside their boats.

GO FISH MOBILE

Materials: Colored construction paper, scissors, hole punch, string, glue, long stick (optional).

Preparation: Make patterns for a large fishhook and small fish.

Activity: Children trace and cut out a fishhook, then several small fish. Help them punch a hole in the top of the hook and tie on a piece of string. They can glue the fish on their hooks themselves. Hang the mobiles from a ceiling fixture, or tie them to a stick for a fishing pole.

remove ends of box and cut along one fold

fold and staple

let children decorate

glue down sponge for a seat

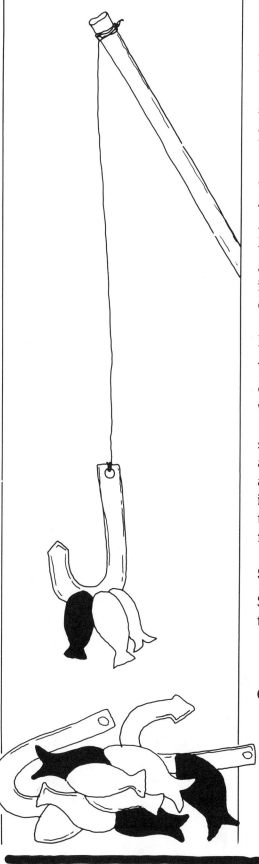

MUSIC AND MOVEMENT ACTIVITIES

BACKYARD TENT

Drape a blanket or sheet over a table for a tent, or make a cardboard tent out of an appliance box as described in the Camping Tent project.

The children crawl in and out of the play tent. If you have some camping equipment, such as a sleeping bag, canteen, and flashlight, let the children use these on their make-believe camping trip.

CATCHING FISH

The children choose partners. One child is the fisher, who pretends to put bait on an imaginary fishing pole, then casts the line into the water. The other child is a fish who wriggles and squirms all over the floor. The fish watches the fisher as it moves about. When the fishing pole jerks, the fish is caught! The fish runs over and gives the fisher a big hug.

FLASHLIGHT ON! FLASHLIGHT OFF!

You'll need a lightweight flashlight for this game. The children form a circle. Send one child to the middle of the circle with the flashlight. Turn out the lights.

The child with the flashlight beams it on another player standing in the circle. That child does a pantomime of some activity related to camping—pitching a tent, hiking, paddling a canoe, cooking over a fire or on an outdoor grill, getting into a sleeping bag—while the rest of the players try to guess the activity. Make sure each child has a turn holding the flashlight and performing.

SONG: "A-Camping We Will Go"

Sing this song to the tune of "The Farmer in the Dell." Ask the children to suggest verses.

> A-camping we will go, a-camping we will go
> Hi-ho, the derrio, a-camping we will go.

Other verses:

> We unpack the car...
> Daddy pitches the tent...
> Mommy starts the fire...
> Our hamburgers taste so good...
> It's getting very dark...
> The stars are coming out...
> We sleep in sleeping bags...

WHAT'S IN MY BACKPACK?

Pack a duffle bag or backpack with a toothbrush, comb, bathing suit, beach thongs, blue jeans, and other items a child might take on a camping trip.

The children take turns looking inside the bag or pack and selecting an object to pantomime. The others try to guess the object.

ROW THE BOAT

Sing "Row, Row, Row the Boat" as the children stand in the formation described below and coordinate their movements. The formation requires six or more children.

The children line up in train fashion. The first and last children move to either side of the line to represent the oars on the rowboat or the paddles on the canoe.

When an oar or paddle bends at the waist, the boat moves forward. When the oar or paddle stands straight, the boat stops. See if the oars or paddles can coordinate their movements and get a rhythm going so the boat can glide smoothly in the water.

You might have the children make the life jackets described in the Safety unit and ask them to wear the jackets during this activity.

BOOKS TO READ ALOUD

Berenstain, Stan and Jan. *The Berenstain Bears Go to Camp.* Random House, 1982.

Brown, Myra Berry. *Pip Camps Out.* Golden Gate, 1966.

Carrick, Carol and David. *Sleep Out.* Seabury Press, 1973.

Parish, Peggy. *Amelia Bedelia Goes Camping.* Greenwillow, 1985.

Rockwell, Anne and Harlow. *The Night We Slept Outside.* Macmillan, 1983.

Schick, Eleanor. *Katie Goes to Camp.* Macmillan, 1968.

Williams, Vera. *Three Days on a River in a Red Canoe.* Greenwillow, 1981.

Chapter Three:

Children Wonder

BEING SICK

Doctor visits are an ordinary part of childhood. Nevertheless, many children are apprehensive, some at the prospect of needles, others about taking their clothes off. When children actually get sick, their anxieties only mount.

Help prepare children for an eventual checkup, illness, or hospital stay. Read stories about other children's real or fictional experiences to help clear up misconceptions and relieve fears. Then follow up with some art and movement activities. Children love to play doctor, and they may work through many of their worries this way, too.

ART ACTIVITIES

MY DOLL IS SICK IN BED

Materials: Shoebox, paint, foam padding (ask for scraps at a carpet store), fabric, tissues, stapler, buttons, yarn, glue.
Preparation: Cut the foam padding to fit in the bottom of the shoebox. Cut a square of fabric to be folded in half and stuffed for a pillow. Cut another piece of fabric for a blanket.
Activity: Children paint their shoeboxes. While the paint dries, they can construct doll pillows. Help them fold a square of fabric in half and staple along the bottom and the open side, leaving an open end. Give them tissues to stuff inside until they have fat, fluffy pillows, then staple closed the open end.

The children make their doll's bed by placing the foam pad mattress in the bottom of the box and tucking in a fabric blanket. The pillow goes at the head of the bed. The children can further decorate the outside of their beds with buttons, fabric scraps, and yarn.

MEDICINE DROPPER PAINTING

Materials: Medicine droppers, paper, thin paint.
Activity: Children fill medicine droppers with paint, then squeeze drops of paint on paper to make a design.

AMBULANCE

Materials: Block of styrofoam, oaktag, toothpicks, red pom-pon or bead, glue.

cut foam to fit box

fold fabric and staple-
leave one end open

add blanket and pillow
to decorated bed

Preparation: Cut out four oaktag wheels for each child.
Activity: Children attach wheels to their styrofoam ambulances with toothpicks. They glue a red pompon or bead on top for a flashing signal light. Their own voices are the ambulance sirens.

DOCTOR'S BAG

Materials: Brown grocery bag, scissors, yarn, hole punch, cotton balls, cotton swabs, tissues, tongue depressors or Popsicle sticks, gauze pads, adhesive tape.
Preparation: Cut the brown bag down to a foot high. Cut off a two-foot length of yarn.
Activity: Children punch a hole in each side of the bag. Help them tie the yarn through the holes to make a handle. The children can place all the tongue depressors, swabs, and other supplies in the bag and "play doctor" with them, or they can reserve some of the materials to decorate the outside of their bags.

DOCTOR'S STETHOSCOPE

Materials: Oaktag, scissors, yarn, stapler, colored markers, empty toilet paper tube.
Preparation: Cut a large oval shape out of oaktag. Cut into the perimeter about an inch at one narrow end, and continue around until you have cut out the center. Widen the slit where you originally cut into the oval. Cut off a foot-long piece of yarn. Cut an inch-wide ring off the toilet paper tube.
Activity: Help the children staple the ends of the yarn a few inches apart at the bottom of their oval frame (opposite the small opening). Let the children decorate their tube rings (scopes) with colored markers. Center the yarn on top of the scope and staple.

If the children have made doctors' bags, they can put their stethoscopes inside.

HOSPITAL

Materials: Half-pint milk or cream container, construction paper, scissors, tape, colored markers, sugar cubes.
Preparation: Cut the top off the half-pint container. Turn it upside down. Cover the top and sides with construction paper and tape it in place.
Activity: Children first draw windows and doors on their hospital, then they glue sugar cube bricks around these architectural features.

SURGICAL MASK

Materials: White construction paper, scissors, white yarn, stapler.

Activity: Children cut rectangles large enough to cover their noses and mouths out of the white paper. They also cut out four 18-inch pieces of yarn. Help them staple the piece of yarn to the corners of the rectangle, then tie on their surgical masks.

ARM IN A CAST

Materials: White construction paper 9″ x 12″, scissors, masking tape, colored markers.

Activity: Children fold their paper in half lengthwise, then wrap it around an arm and wrist. Fasten the cast on each child's arm with masking tape. The children sign their names on each other's casts with markers.

BED TRAY

Materials: Cardboard box, scissors, colored markers or crayons, clear contact paper.

Preparation: Remove the lid or top panels off the box and turn it upside down. Cut out a large arc on both long side panels of the box as shown. The cutout area should be large enough to fit comfortably over a child's lap.

Activity: Children decorate the tops of their bed trays with markers or crayons. Protect the artwork and the cardboard surface by covering it with clear contact paper.

MUSIC AND MOVEMENT ACTIVITIES

SONG: "Just a Spoonful of Medicine"

Sing your own verse to the tune of "Just a Spoonful of Sugar Helps the Medicine Go Down," the song from the movie *Mary Poppins*. Just substitute a different complaint— stomach ache, cold, flu, sore throat.

> Just a spoonful of medicine helps the sore throat go away,
> The sore throat go away, the sore throat go away.
> Just a spoonful of medicine helps the sore throat go away,
> I'm feeling better every day!

attach yarn to mask then tie on each child's mask

remove top panels and turn box upside down

cut out a large arc on each side

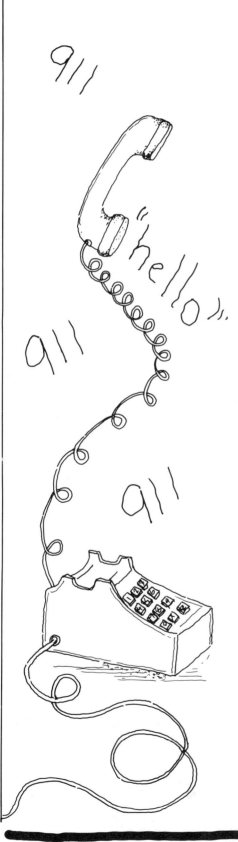

EMERGENCY 9-1-1

Let the children practice calling for an ambulance on a toy telephone. Suggest what the children should do and say in such an emergency: "Pretend you need an ambulance for a sick or hurt person. Dial 9-1-1 on the toy telephone. When the dispatcher answers the phone, you say, 'This is an emergency. My grandma fell. Send an ambulance to 135 Willow Street.'"

BEANBAG PILLOWS

The children pretend beanbags are little pillows. First they put their heads on the pillows. Then they walk with the pillows on their heads, shoulders, necks.

SICK DAYS

Ask the children what they do when they're home sick. As the children answer, everybody acts out the responses. Possible responses are sleep in bed, watch television, take medicine, read a story.

MY BLANKET

Ask the children to bring in their favorite blanket from home. Have extra blankets or bath towels on hand for those who forget. The children pretend to be sick at home and cover themselves with their blankets. What else might their blankets be? The children act out their ideas—a tent, an umbrella, a cape, a sleeping bag.

BOOKS TO READ ALOUD

Bemelmans, Ludwig. *Madeline*. Penguin, 1977.
Berenstain, Stan and Jan. *The Berenstain Bears Go to the Doctor*. Random House, 1981.
Berger, Knute, Robert A. Tidwell and Margaret Haseltine. *A Visit to the Doctor*. Grosset and Dunlap, 1960.
Brandenberg, F. *I Wish I Was Sick Too*. Greenwillow, 1976.
Breinburg, Petronella. *Doctor Shawn*. Crowell, 1975.
Chalmers, Mary. *Come to the Doctor, Harry*. Harper and Row, 1981.
Charlip, Remy and Burton Supree. *Mother, Mother I Feel Sick; Send for the Doctor Quick, Quick, Quick!* Four Winds Press, 1966.

Delton, Judy. *Groundhog's Day at the Doctor.* Parent's Magazine Press, 1981.

Galbraith, K. *Spots Are Special.* Atheneum, 1976.

Greenwald, Arthur and Barry Head. *Going to the Hospital.* Family Communications, 1977.

_____ . *Having an Operation.* Family Communications, 1977.

_____ . *Wearing a Cast.* Family Communications, 1977.

Hann, J. *Up Day, Down Day.* Scholastic, 1978.

Hurd, Edith T. *Johnny Lion's Bad Day.* Harper and Row, 1970.

MacLachian, P. *The Sick Day.* Random House, 1979.

Maestro, G. *Leopard Is Sick.* Greenwillow, 1978.

Mao-chiug, Chang. *The Little Doctor.* Foreign Languages Press, 1965.

Marino, B. *Eric Needs Stitches.* Addison-Wesley, 1979.

Raskin, E. *Spectacles.* Atheneum, 1968.

Reit, Seymour. *Jenny's in the Hospital.* Western, 1984.

Rey, Margret. *Curious George Goes to the Hospital.* Houghton Mifflin, 1966.

Robison, Deborah and Carla Perez, M.D. *Your Turn, Doctor.* Dial, 1982.

Rockwell, Harlow. *My Doctor.* Macmillan, 1982.

Virin, Anna. *Elsa's Bears Need the Doctor.* Harvey House, 1978.

Wahl, J. *Doctor Rabbit.* Delacorte, 1970.

Weber, Alfons. *Elizabeth Gets Well.* Crowell, 1969.

Wolde, Gunilla. *Betsy and the Doctor.* Random House, 1978.

_____ . *Betsy and the Chicken Pox.* Random House, 1976.

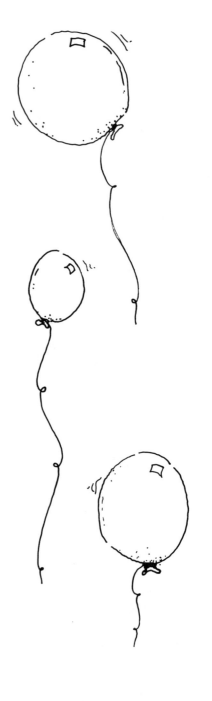

MOVING AWAY

According to the 1983 Employee Relocation Council, one in five American families moves each year. Although moving can be exciting, it is also a stressful time for children and their families. Small children are confused as they see their belongings disappear into boxes and walk through the empty rooms. They are anxious about having to part with friends.

Listening to stories about other children's experiences and feelings about moving will help your children cope with the idea, and some with the actual situation. Follow up with art, music, and movement activities that present moving as an adventure.

ART ACTIVITIES

VAN FULL OF FURNITURE

Materials: Shoebox, paint, paintbrush, black poster board, scissors, brass paper fasteners, colored markers, bottle caps, glue.

Activity: Children paint the outside of their shoeboxes. Next they paint a pair of bottle caps yellow for headlights and another pair red for brake lights. Then they cut four wheels out of the black poster board.

When the paint is dry, the children turn their shoeboxes upside down and attach the wheels with brass fasteners. They can cut fold-out doors on either side of their moving vans, and windows in the front and on the sides above the doors. The headlight bottle caps are glued on the front of the van, the brake light caps on the rear. Provide markers for any other decoration.

MOVING BOXES, BOXES, BOXES!

Materials: Variety of small boxes, glue, paint, paintbrush.

Activity: Children arrange the boxes on top of one another any way they like and glue them in place. When the glue is dry, they can paint their box sculptures.

add red and yellow bottle caps

add doors, moving company, etc.

JOE'S MOVING VAN

NEW ROOMS

Materials: Shoeboxes, old magazines and catalogs, scissors, glue.

Activity: Children look through magazines and mail order catalogs to find pictures of furniture and objects for different rooms in a new home. They cut out the pictures and sort them according to room (bedroom, living room, family room, etc.).

Have the children remove the lids on the shoeboxes and stack the boxes on their sides. Designate each box as a different room. Now the children can glue the cutouts inside the shoebox rooms. If they like, they can staple the boxes together at the end to make a whole house or apartment full of rooms.

MOVING BOX RUBBINGS

Materials: Pieces of corrugated cardboard, scissors, newsprint or other lightweight paper, masking tape, crayons (the kind with flat sides are best).

Preparation: Cut pieces of corrugated cardboard into different geometric shapes. Peel off the top layer of paper to uncover the corrugated (rippled) layer below. Tape the shapes on a table within an area no larger than the size paper the children will be working with. Peel the paper labels off some crayons.

Activity: Children place their papers on top of the shapes and rub over them with the broad side of a crayon. An impression of the corrugated shapes will appear on their papers.

PACK YOUR SUITCASES

Materials: Small rectangular box (ask a local optician for an eyeglass box), paint, paintbrush, yarn or heavy string, colored markers.

Activity: Children paint their suitcase boxes whatever color they like. When the paint is dry, attach a yarn or string handle to each child's suitcase. Then let the children further decorate their cases with colored markers. They may want to pack small doll clothes inside.

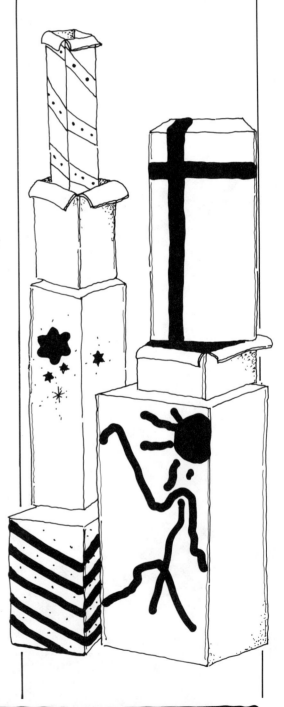

OLD HOME, NEW HOME

Materials: Two brown grocery bags, scissors, paint, paintbrush.

Activity: Turn the grocery bags upside down so the open ends rest on the floor. Help the children cut a fold-out door in each bag building. Then have them paint the door and some windows on each home. Label one bag Old Home and the other New Home.

MY NEW HOUSE

Materials: Colored construction paper, scissors, glue, crayons.

Preparation: Cut out a variety of shapes from different colors of construction paper.

Activity: Give each child a whole sheet of construction paper. Set out the shape cutouts, glue, and crayons. The children arrange and glue the cutouts on the background sheet to construct a new house (or apartment building). They can add architectural details and landscaping with crayons.

MUSIC AND MOVEMENT ACTIVITIES

WHAT ARE YOU MOVING?

Partners pretend to be movers. The children perform a pantomime together, pretending to lift different things into the moving van. The movers must lift heavy boxes, light boxes, the refrigerator, a bed, a box full of china, a lamp, and so on.

FOLLOW THE MOVING VAN

One child, the leader, pretends to be the driver of a moving van. If you have a set of road signs, place them around the room; if not, pin road signs (stop sign, traffic lights, one way arrow, detour arrow) on several other children and station them in various parts of the room. The rest of the children must follow the moving van around the room, driving their own pretend cars. When the line of vehicles reaches a road sign, the drivers must act accordingly.

WHAT'S INSIDE?

Place several objects (such as a book, cup, radio, hairbrush) inside a large cardboard box. The children take turns looking inside the box, touching an object, and doing a pantomime to help the others guess what the object is. After they have guessed correctly, everybody performs the pantomime together.

MOVING WITH HOOPS

Each child needs a hoop to act out the following suggestions: "Wrap newspaper around the glassware. (*Swivel hips to make hoop circle around your waist.*) Pack a box with lots of things. (*Place hoop on floor and jump in and out.*) Carry the sofa out of the house. (*Partners hold hoop on opposite sides and walk around.*) Pack up the van. (*Roll the hoop.*) Drive the van to your new home. (*Turn hoop like a steering wheel.*) Honk your horn. (*Say "Beep!"*) Slow down for the red light. (*Lower hoop to floor and sit inside it.*) Green light—you can go again! (*Pick up hoop and steer again.*)"

ECHOES IN THE EMPTY HOUSE

Discuss how empty houses make echoes. Let the children take turns saying a sentence that the others will echo. Then have all the children act out the sentence. For example, if a child says "I love ice cream," the others echo or repeat the sentence, then pretend to lick ice cream cones.

FURNITURE PEOPLE

Several children pretend to be furniture in a new living room that needs arranging. One child can be a sofa, another a lamp, another a table. The rest of the children must crawl *under* the table, *over* the sofa, around the lamp. After five minutes, the children switch roles.

BOOKS TO READ ALOUD

Adshead, Gladys L. *Brownies—They're Moving!* Henry Z. Walck, 1970.

Berenstain, Stan and Jan. *The Berenstain Bears' Moving Day.* Random House, 1981.

Brown, Myra B. *Pip Moves Away.* Children's Press, 1967.

Fisher, Aileen. *Best Little House.* Crowell, 1966.

Hickman, Martha W. *I'm Moving.* Abingdon Press, 1979.

Hughes. *Moving Molly.* Prentice-Hall, 1978.

Isadora, Rachel. *The Potter's Kitchen.* Greenwillow, 1977.

Iwasaki, Chikiro. *Will You Be My Friend?* McGraw Hill, 1970.

Jones, Penelope. *I'm Not Moving!* Bradbury Press, 1980.

Kantrowitz, Mildred. *Good-bye, Kitchen.* Parent's Magazine Press, 1972.

Keats, Ezra Jack. *The Trip.* Greenwillow, 1978.

Marino, Dorothy. *Moving Day.* Dial, 1963.

Tobias, Tobi. *Moving Day.* Knopf, 1976.

Viklund, Alice R. *Moving Away.* McGraw Hill, 1967.

Waber, Bernard. *The House on East 88th Street.* Houghton Mifflin, 1978.

Watson, Wendy. *Moving.* Crowell, 1978.

Wise, William. *The House with the Red Roof.* Putnam, 1961.

Zolotow, Charlotte. *Janey.* Harper and Row, 1973.

SLEEPING AT NIGHT

remove flaps and one side panel

Many small children need reassuring at night. Some have nightmares in which they are threatened by monsters or other composites of their imaginations; others simply don't like the dark. Activities that encourage the children to make friends with the monsters and find comfort in the dark may help them come to terms with their nighttime fears.

ART ACTIVITIES

ME IN THE DARK

Materials: Drawing paper, crayons, thinned black paint, paintbrush, newspapers.
Activity: Children draw self-portraits on paper with crayons. Recommend light rather than dark color crayons, and tell the children that any areas they want to appear white must actually be crayoned white. After their drawings are complete, the children place them on newspaper and brush the thinned black paint over the portraits. The crayon resists the watery mixture, so the drawing will show through the black paint.

NIGHTTIME DIORAMA

Materials: Cardboard box, scissors, black and green paint, paintbrushes, construction paper, glue, half-pint milk or cream cartons, modeling clay, twigs.
Preparation: Cut off the top flaps on the box. Set the box on one side and cut off the panel on the opposite side. Cut off the tops of the half-pint cartons. Take the children on a walk to collect twigs.
Activity: Children paint the inside walls of the box black and the floor of the box green. They glue construction paper on the outside surfaces of the half-pint cartons, then cut out or draw windows and doors.

When the paint is dry, the children glue the carton houses down on the green floor of the box. They cut out construction paper stars and a moon, and glue them to the black walls. They stick twigs in small balls of clay and press them onto the floor of the box between the houses. The finished effect is a miniature town at night.

Remove tops from ½ pint cartons and glue construction paper to outside surfaces

FRIENDLY FURRY MONSTERS

Materials: Styrofoam cup, fur and felt scraps, yarn (curly or coarsely spun is best), glue, glue brush, plastic eyes with moving eyeballs (available at fabric or crafts stores) or buttons.
Preparation: Cut the fur, felt, and yarn into small pieces.
Activity: Children turn their styrofoam cups upside down and brush glue all over them. They stick fur, felt scraps, or yarn on the tacky surface. When the cup is covered, they glue plastic eyes or button eyes on their monsters. Some monsters may want to sport a felt hat or hair ribbon.

MY NIGHTGOWN OR PAJAMAS

Materials: Oaktag, scissors, flannel and knit fabric scraps, buttons, glue.
Preparation: Cut a nightgown or pajamas pattern out of oaktag.
Activity: Children trace the pajamas pattern onto another piece of oaktag and cut it out. They glue pieces of flannel or other soft fabric and buttons on their pajamas.

INK BLOT DARKNESS

Materials: Paper, black paint, medicine dropper, marker.
Activity: Children fold their papers in half, then open them again. They squeeze several drops of paint on one side of the fold, then refold and press down on the paper with their hands. When they reopen the paper, they will find a dark symmetrical blot. Ask the children to describe the darkness they made. Write the child's exact words on the picture with the marker.

STAR AND MOON MOBILE

Materials: Oaktag, scissors, glue, silver and gold glitter, wire coat hanger.
Preparation: Cut star and moon patterns out of oaktag.
Activity: Children trace and cut several stars and a moon out of oaktag. They spread glue on the cutouts and sprinkle on glitter—gold for the moon, silver for the stars—then shake off any excess glitter. Punch holes in the cutouts and suspend them on strings tied to the wire hanger.

DREAM BED

Materials: Matchbox, paint, paintbrush, fabric, cotton, stapler.

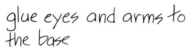

glue one lid to the other

Preparation: Discard the top of the matchbox. You only need the inside box that slides out. Cut out a fabric square whose sides are the same width as the short side of the box. Cut out another fabric piece the same dimensions as the bottom of the box.

Activity: Children paint the outside of the box the color of their own beds if they like. Help them make pillows by folding the fabric square in half and stapling along two sides. After the children stuff their pillows with cotton, you can staple the third side closed. The children make their beds by putting the pillow at the head and tucking in the other piece of fabric as a blanket.

MISTER MONSTER

Materials: Egg carton, scissors, glue, paint, pipe cleaners.

Preparation: Cut the lid off the egg carton, then cut the lid in half widthwise. Cut out two egg cup sections for eyes. Cut out two pointy dividers for arms. Glue one lid half on top of the other so that the inside edges are touching.

Activity: Children glue egg section eyes on whichever lid half is faceup. Divider arms are glued on either side of the construction. When the glue dries, the children paint their monsters however they like. They can glue pipe cleaners on top of the monster's head for antennae or some other monster feature.

glue eyes and arms to the base

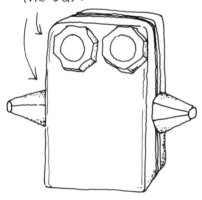

MUSIC AND MOVEMENT ACTIVITIES

SONG: "Are You Sleeping?"

Sing this song to the tune of "Frere Jacques," repeating until you have sung each child's name.

> Are you sleeping, are you sleeping
> My friend Jamie, my friend Ann?
> Now you know it's night time.
> Turn out all the lights time.
> Dream sweet dreams.
> Sweet, sweet dreams.

NAME YOUR MONSTER

The children pretend to be all kinds of monsters. Each child takes a turn showing the others how to be a friendly monster, angry monster, scary monster, lovable monster, or any other kind of monster they feel like being. The others imitate the movement, then try to think of a good name for the monster—Big Tooth, Mad Maddie, Mister Creeps, Gentle George. Ask if any of the children have dreams about monsters. Are the monsters friendly or frightening in their dreams?

GET READY FOR BED

Have the children act out their bedtime routines. Call out each step: "Take off your clothes. Fill the bathtub with water. Take your bath. Wash your hair. Soap up your body. Now rinse off. Get out of the tub and dry off with a towel. Put on your pajamas. Brush your teeth. Dry your hair with a blow dryer. Pull down your bedspread and blankets. Hop into bed. Mom or Dad shuts the light. Close your eyes and go to sleep!"

BOOKS TO READ ALOUD

Babbitt, Natalie. *The Something.* Farrar, Straus and Giroux, 1970.
Barrett, Judi. *I Hate to Go to Bed Book.* Four Winds Press, 1977.
Bradbury, Ray. *Switch On Night.* Pantheon, 1955.
Brown, Margaret W. *Goodnight Moon.* Harper and Row, 1947.
Crowe, Robert L. *Clyde Monster.* Dutton, 1976.
Drescher, Henrik. *Simon's Book.* Lothrop, Lee and Shepard, 1983.
Hayward, Linda. *I Had a Bad Dream.* Western, 1985.
Hoban, Russell. *Bedtime for Frances.* Harper and Row, 1960.
Hill, Susan. *Go Away Bad Dreams.* Random House, 1984.
Levine, Joan G. *A Bedtime Story.* Dutton, 1975.
Mayer, Mercer. *There's a Nightmare in My Closet.* Dial, 1976.
Memling, Carl. *What's in the Dark?* Parent's Magazine Press, 1971.
Peck, Richard. *Monster Night at Grandma's House.* Viking, 1981.
Plath, Sylvia. *The Bed Book.* Harper and Row, 1976.
Sendak, Maurice. *In the Night Kitchen.* Harper and Row, 1970.
——————— . *Where the Wild Things Are.* Harper and Row, 1963.
Sharmat, Marjorie. *Goodnight Andrew, Goodnight Craig.* Harper and Row, 1969.
Viorst, Judith. *My Mama Says There Aren't Any Zombies, Ghosts, Vampires, Creatures, Demons, Monsters, Friends, Goblins or Things.* Atheneum, 1973.
Virin, Anna. *Elsa in the Night.* Harvey House, 1974.
Zagone, Theresa. *No Nap for Me.* Dutton, 1978.
Zolotow, Charlotte. *Sleepy Book.* Lothrop, Lee and Shepard, 1958.

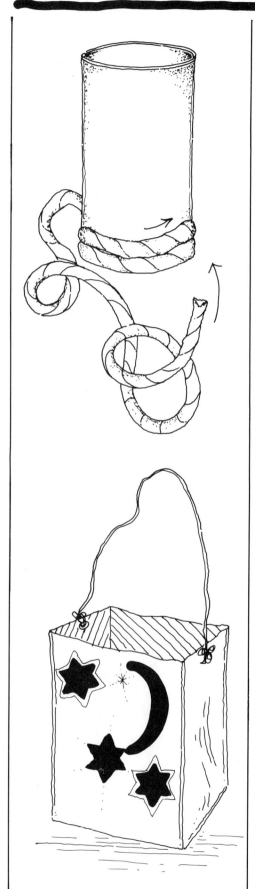

STARTING SCHOOL

During their first days at nursery school or preschool, many children are apprehensive. You can make them feel more comfortable and confident in their new surroundings with stories and follow-up activities that describe what they will be doing at school.

ART ACTIVITIES

PENCIL HOLDER

Materials: Empty frozen juice container, glue, thick yarn (the kind used for wrapping gifts), scissors.
Activity: Children squeeze glue all around the outside of the juice can, then wrap yarn around in close coils until the can is covered.

SCHOOL CHILDREN COLLAGE

Materials: Old magazines, back-to-school sale catalogs and toy catalogs, scissors, oaktag, glue.
Activity: Children search through magazines and catalogs for pictures of school-age children like themselves and cut them out. They arrange the cutouts in a collage on oaktag, then glue them in place.

BAG FOR PROJECTS

Materials: Brown grocery bag, hole punch, yarn, colored construction paper, scissors, glue.
Preparation: Punch holes on opposite sides at the top of the bag. Tie the end of a piece of yarn through each hole to form a handle.
Activity: Children cut shapes out of construction paper and glue the pieces all over the outside of their bags. They use the bags to take home art projects during the year.

THE CHILDREN ON THE BUS

Materials: Yellow poster board, scissors, markers, small paper plates, crayons, yarn, glue.
Preparation: Make a large school bus out of poster board. Write School Bus across the broad side of the bus. Cut out windows.
Activity: Children draw their own faces on paper plates, then glue on yarn hair, eyebrows, and eyelashes. Staple each self-portrait behind a window.

MY LUNCH BOX

Materials: Construction paper, scissors, old magazines with regular food features (for example, *Good Housekeeping* or *Family Circle*), glue.

Preparation: Fold a piece of construction paper in half. Cut along the open ends to form a lunch box handle as shown. Cut a thermos out of a different color piece of construction paper.

Activity: Children look through magazines for pictures of nutritious lunch foods or snacks and cut them out. They open the lunch box at the handle, and glue the cutouts and the thermos inside. They can decorate the outside of their lunch boxes with construction paper shapes they cut out themselves.

MUSIC AND MOVEMENT ACTIVITIES

SONG: "This is the Way We Walk to School"

Sing these verses to the tune of "Here We Go Round the Mulberry Bush" as the children perform the actions.

> This is the way we walk to school
> Walk to school, walk to school.
> This is the way we walk to school
> So early in the morning.

Other verses:

> This is the way we hop to school...
> This is the way we gallop to school...
> This is the way we skate to school...
> This is the way we run to school...
> This is the way we bike to school...
> This is the way we drive to school...

MUSICAL SCHOOL CHAIRS

Line up chairs, alternately facing forward and backward. Start with a chair for each child in your group. As you play music on a record or tape player, have the children circle around the chairs. When the music stops, the children scramble for a seat. Remove a chair and repeat, as you would for a regular game of musical chairs, but *never eliminate a child*. The children without chairs when the music stops can sit on laps, touch a remaining chair, pretend to be a chair.

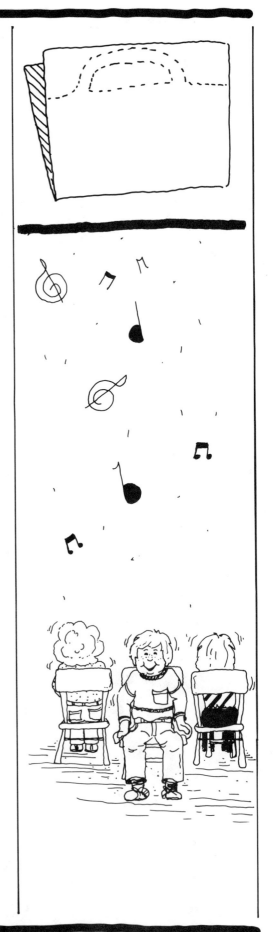

staple self-portraits behind windows

SONG: "The Wheels on the Bus"

Sing this old favorite with a few adaptations as your children pretend to be on a school bus.

> The wheels on the bus go round and round
> Round and round, round and round.
> The wheels on the bus go round and round
> On the way to school.

Other verses:

> The horn on the bus goes beep, beep, beep...
> The doors on the bus open and close...
> The windows on the bus go up and down...
> The children on the bus say "I love school!"

SCHOOL BELL IS RINGING!

The children move freely in a large open area. When you ring a bell, the children must freeze—pretending to be a stationary object in the classroom, such as a table, chair, block, or easel. When the bell stops ringing, the children move around once again. Continue playing until the children begin to lose interest. You might let them take turns ringing the bell.

BOOKS TO READ ALOUD

Amoss, Berthe. *The Very Worst Thing.* Parent's Magazine Press, 1972.

Bemelmans, Ludwig. *Madeline.* Viking, 1939.

Berenstain, Stan and Jan. *The Berenstain Bears Go to School.* Random House, 1978.

Bizen, Bill. *First Day in School.* Doubleday, 1972.

Breinburg, Petronella. *Shawn Goes to School.* Crowell, 1973.

Charles, Donald. *Calico Cat at School.* Children's Press, 1981.

Chorao, Kay. *Molly's Lies.* Houghton Mifflin, 1979.

Cohen, Miriam. *Best Friends.* Macmillan, 1971.

————. *Tough Jim.* Macmillan, 1974.

————. *Will I Have a Friend?* Macmillan, 1967.

Hurd, Edith T. *Come with Me to Nursery School.* Coward-McCann, 1970.

Isadora, Rachel. *Willaby.* Macmillan, 1977.

Kantrowitz, Mildred. *Willy Bear.* Four Winds Press, 1980.

Lenski, Lois. *Debbie Goes to Nursery School.* Henry Z. Walch, 1970.

————. *A Dog Came to School.* Henry Z. Walch, 1955.

Marino, Dorothy. *Buzzy Bear's First Day at School.* Watts, Franklin, 1970.

Reif, Patricia. *The First Day of School.* Western, 1981.

Rockwell, Harlow. *My Nursery School.* Greenwillow, 1976.

Schwartz, Amy. *Bea and Mr. Jones.* Bradbury Press, 1982.

Serfozo, Mary. *Welcome Roberto.* Follett, 1969.

Surowiecki, Sandra. *Joshua's Day.* Lollipop Power, 1972.

Udry, Janice M. *What Mary Jo Shared.* Albert Whitman, 1966.

Wells, Rosemary. *Timothy Goes to School.* Dial, 1981.

Yashima, Taro. *Crow Boy.* Viking, 1955.

STAYING SAFE

Children ages three to five are old enough to understand the importance of safety and to appreciate your concern for their safety. Incorporate this assortment of activities in your discussions about sidewalk and street safety, car safety, bike safety, water safety, and product safety (what's safe to eat and what's poisonous).

ART ACTIVITIES

SAFE TO EAT

Materials: Red construction paper, scissors, magazines, glue.
Preparation: Cut a big open mouth out of red paper, or make a pattern for the children to trace and cut out. Also cut out or make a pattern for a closed mouth.
Activity: Children look through magazines and cut out pictures of things that are safe to eat (foods, candy, vitamins) and not safe to eat (plants, household cleansers, small toys such as beads). They glue the safe items on the open mouth, and the unsafe items on the closed mouth.

MY BIKE

Materials: Construction paper, scissors, glue, glitter, narrow ribbon.
Preparation: Cut a bicycle out of construction paper, or make a pattern for the children to trace and cut out themselves. Cut off small pieces of ribbon.
Activity: Children glue glitter on their bicycles and ribbon streamers on the handlebars.

SIDEWALK FUN

Materials: Black and white construction paper, scissors, magazines, glue.
Preparation: Cut out a wide strip of white construction paper.
Activity: Children glue the white paper strip along the bottom of a sheet of black construction paper to make a sidewalk and street. They look through magazines and catalogs and cut out pictures of people doing sidewalk-type activities—riding a bike, walking, pushing a stroller, playing with a ball, roller skating. They glue the cutouts on the white sidewalk strip. If they like, they can also cut out cars and other road vehicles to glue on the street.

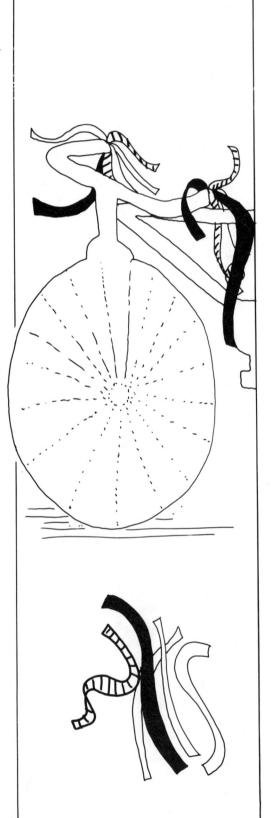

FASTEN YOUR SEAT BELTS

Materials: Poster board, scissors, magazines, glue.
Preparation: Cut out a poster board seat belt. Cut slots on the buckle ends so the belt can really fasten around the child's waist.
Activity: Children look through magazines and cut out pictures of vehicles (cars, trucks, buses, motorcycles). Perhaps they'll be lucky enough to find a public service message about seat belts! The children glue the cutouts on their seat belts, then put them around their waists and fasten them.

STOP AND GO

Materials: Colored construction paper, scissors, glue.
Preparation: If the children cannot cut out their own shapes, then cut out a black rectangle and red, yellow, and green circles for each child.
Activity: Children construct traffic lights by gluing the color circles on the black rectangle—red on top, yellow in the middle, and green on the bottom.

LIFE JACKET FOR BOATING

Materials: Large brown grocery bag, scissors, hole punch, yarn or shoelaces, orange or yellow construction paper, glue.
Preparation: Open the grocery bag and turn it upside down. Slit up the middle of one wide side of the bag (the front of the jacket). Continue cutting into the top, removing a large enough area for a neck hole, but leaving shoulders. Cut armholes out of the top and narrow panels.
Activity: Children punch two holes on each side of the opening in the front of the life jacket. Knot the yarn or lace. Show each child how to lace the jacket by inserting the yarn through the bottom left hole, up through the top left hole, down through the top right hole, and up through the bottom right hole. Then the children can decorate their jackets by gluing on pieces of orange or yellow construction paper.

If a child cannot lace, staple two ribbons onto each side of the opening for ties. Ties are also better if the children want to actually get in and out of their life jackets as they pretend to row a boat or paddle a canoe.

save ✡ lives ✡

let children decorate their seat belts

show children how to lace

MUSIC AND MOVEMENT ACTIVITIES

SAFETY WALK

Place masking tape on the floor to make a road all around the room. As the children walk along the road, call out imaginary things in their path—a stop sign, a stranger, a berry bush. Ask, "What do you do when you see this?" Review safety rules and resume the walk.

BUCKLE UP!

Arrange chairs as the front and back seats in an automobile. When the children pretend to climb in the car, remind them to "Buckle up!" They can make the motions or fasten the seat belts they made themselves. Then they can go on a pretend drive.

MR. YUM AND MR. YUK

For this safety game, you'll need happy face stickers, Mr. Yuk stickers (available by writing to the Department of Health and Human Services), and materials for making product labels (paper, pen, and masking tape).

   One child pretends to be smart Mr. Yum, who identifies good things to eat. Another child is Mr. Yuk, who identifies things that are poisonous. Tape picture labels on the rest of the children. The labels should include products that are edible and items that are unsafe or poisonous to eat. For example, you might label the children as spaghetti, ice cream, bananas, a can of paint, a bottle of medicine, and a bottle of bleach.

   Mr. Yum and Mr. Yuk place their "mark"—a sticker—on the appropriate labels. Although Mr. Yum and Mr. Yuk do the sticking, all the children participate in deciding which sticker to use by calling out "Yum!" or "Yuk!" when you point to a label.

BICYCLING LEGS

The children lie on their backs, hoist up their hips, and bicycle in the air with their legs. Narrate as they bike along: "You're biking to the street corner. You stop and look both ways. (*Children pause and move their heads right and left.*) No cars! It's okay to cross the street, but walk your bike, don't ride it. Now you're on the sidewalk across the street. You can start biking again. (*Children resume bicycling.*)"

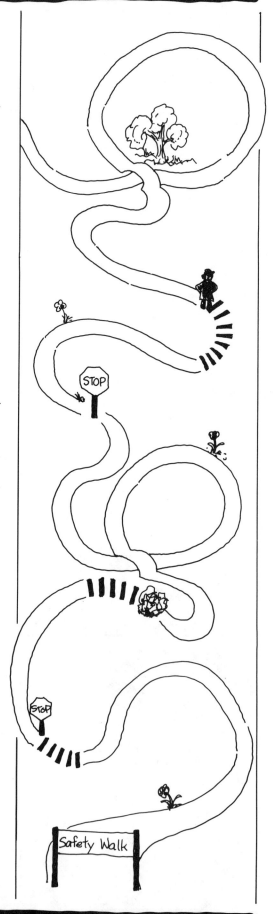

SONG: "Five Little Children Swimming in a Pool"

Sing this song to the tune of "Five Little Monkeys."

Five little children swimming in a pool,
One didn't follow the lifeguard's rule.
The lifeguard blew the whistle and we heard him shout,
"Splashing's not safe, you'll have to get out!"

Other verses:

Four little children. . .
"You jumped in the pool, you'll have to get out!"

Three little children. . .
"You're in too deep, you'll have to get out!"

Two little children. . .
"Your lips are turning blue, you'll have to get out!"

One little child. . .
"Your Mom should be with you, you'll have to get out!"

No little children. . .
They didn't follow the lifeguard's rules. . .
"If you can't swim safely, please stay out!"

BOOKS TO READ ALOUD

Chlad, Dorothy. *When I Ride in a Car.* Children's Press, 1983.
——————. *Poisons Make You Sick.* Children's Press, 1984.
——————. *Bicycles Are Fun to Ride.* Children's Press, 1982.
——————. *Matches, Lighters and Firecrackers Are Not Toys.* Children's Press, 1982.
Kessler, Leonard. *Last One In Is a Rotten Egg.* Harper and Row, 1969.
McLeod, Emilie. *The Bear's Bicycle.* Little, Brown, 1975.
Seuling, Barbara. *Stay Safe, Play Safe.* Western, 1985.
Smaridge, Norah. *Watch Out!* Abingdon Press, 1970.
Viorst, Judith. *Try It Again Sam: Safety When You Walk.* Lothrop, Lee and Shepard, 1970.

ABOUT THE AUTHOR

Lynn Cohen received her B.S. in education from S.U.N.Y. at New Paltz, and M.S. in remedial reading from Johns Hopkins University. Education of children, teachers, college students, and parents has been her main focus for fourteen years. She teaches early childhood and elementary education at S.U.N.Y College at Farmingdale and S.U.N.Y. College at Old Westbury and is an early childhood consultant.